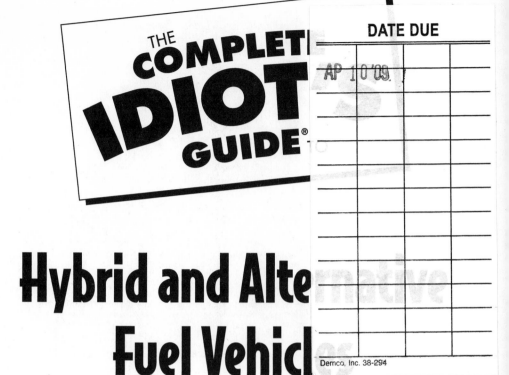

THE COMPLETE IDIOT GUIDE®

Hybrid and Alternative Fuel Vehicles

by Jack R. Nerad

ALPHA

A member of Penguin Group (USA) Inc.

This book is dedicated to my lovely daughters Maddie, Emma, and Greta with the hope that, in a small way at least, it will make their future and the future of all children who live in this world better and more secure.

ALPHA BOOKS

Published by the Penguin Group

Penguin Group (USA) Inc., 375 Hudson Street, New York, New York 10014, USA

Penguin Group (Canada), 90 Eglinton Avenue East, Suite 700, Toronto, Ontario M4P 2Y3, Canada (a division of Pearson Penguin Canada Inc.)

Penguin Books Ltd., 80 Strand, London WC2R 0RL, England

Penguin Ireland, 25 St. Stephen's Green, Dublin 2, Ireland (a division of Penguin Books Ltd.)

Penguin Group (Australia), 250 Camberwell Road, Camberwell, Victoria 3124, Australia (a division of Pearson Australia Group Pty. Ltd.)

Penguin Books India Pvt. Ltd., 11 Community Centre, Panchsheel Park, New Delhi—110 017, India

Penguin Group (NZ), 67 Apollo Drive, Rosedale, North Shore, Auckland 1311, New Zealand (a division of Pearson New Zealand Ltd.)

Penguin Books (South Africa) (Pty.) Ltd., 24 Sturdee Avenue, Rosebank, Johannesburg 2196, South Africa

Penguin Books Ltd., Registered Offices: 80 Strand, London WC2R 0RL, England

International Standard Book Number: 978-1-59257-635-7
Library of Congress Catalog Card Number: 2007922823

09 08 07   8 7 6 5 4 3 2 1

Interpretation of the printing code: The rightmost number of the first series of numbers is the year of the book's printing; the rightmost number of the second series of numbers is the number of the book's printing. For example, a printing code of 07-1 shows that the first printing occurred in 2007.

Printed in the United States of America

Note: This publication contains the opinions and ideas of its author. It is intended to provide helpful and informative material on the subject matter covered. It is sold with the understanding that the author and publisher are not engaged in rendering professional services in the book. If the reader requires personal assistance or advice, a competent professional should be consulted.

The author and publisher specifically disclaim any responsibility for any liability, loss, or risk, personal or otherwise, which is incurred as a consequence, directly or indirectly, of the use and application of any of the contents of this book.

Most Alpha books are available at special quantity discounts for bulk purchases for sales promotions, premiums, fundraising, or educational use. Special books, or book excerpts, can also be created to fit specific needs.

For details, write: Special Markets, Alpha Books, 375 Hudson Street, New York, NY 10014.

Publisher: *Marie Butler-Knight*
Senior Acquisitions Editor: *Paul Dinas*
Managing Editor: *Billy Fields*
Development Editor: *Ginny Munroe*
Production Editor: *Kayla Dugger*
Copy Editor: *Tricia Liebig*
Cover Designer: *Bill Thomas*
Book Designer: *Trina Wurst*
Indexer: *Tonya Heard*
Layout: *Ayanna Lacey*
Proofreader: *Aaron Black*

Contents at a Glance

Contents

Introduction

Few automotive issues are as emotionally charged as the one that surrounds hybrid vehicles. Hybrid vehicles have become a litmus test, an
are-you-with-us-or-are-you-against-us bellwether that has created a
great divide in the automotive world. The debate that surrounds hybrid
and other alternative propulsion systems touches on some of the most
important issues of our time. Included among them are such volatile
topics as global warming, the depletion of fossil fuels, and the situations
in the Middle East. Though they are just another form of personal
transportation, hybrids have become a political symbol, a talisman that
represents things that are good in a world filled with evil. Many who
drive hybrids do it to make a statement, not just about how they see
themselves but also about how they see the world.

The debate on hybrids and alternative fuel vehicles is strident and
ongoing. I can vividly recall a spirited exchange of views among auto
journalists in a tavern outside Frankfurt, Germany, that began with a
discussion of hybrid vehicles and devolved into an argument about big
business, unions, health care, and the peril or fallacy of global warming.
Hybrids seem to engender that kind of passion.

That passion is understandable, because in a way hybrids represent a
single world view, the view that we as citizens of the world are threat-
ened by the imminent exhaustion of our natural resources, by increasingly polluted air and water, and by a climate that is spinning out of
control. Hybrids acknowledge that we and our children and our children's children are under siege, and the enemy, well, the enemy is us.
We are the ones who have wantonly consumed the world's resources,
poured filth into our environs, and sent our very climate reeling.

To many a hybrid vehicle is a symbol of both defiance and hope.
Driving a hybrid isn't just a way to save money on gas, not just a way
to ride alone in the carpool lane on your daily commute. It says, loudly
and clearly, I care about the future and I'm willing to do something
about it.

To those who have already made that stand, I applaud you. It takes
guts to stand out from the norm and do what you believe is the right
thing, no matter what others may think. I am proud that my father,

pushing 80 years of age at the time, was among the first purchasers of a Toyota Prius hybrid, and he made that purchase, as they say, before Priuses were cool. To those who are currently considering a hybrid or alternative fuel vehicle, I salute you as well. I believe you are doing this because you have the right instincts, because you care about your fellow man and your planet, and you're willing to put your money where your mouth is.

With that as background, it would have been very easy and very popular to write an unblushingly flattering portrait of hybrid vehicles and thump the tub that you and everyone else should buy one. It would have been easy to praise them to the skies for their obvious goodness, repeat unchallenged the popular press reports on the threat of global warming, and decry American car manufacturers' seeming reluctance to push forward what is generally regarded as the technology of the future. As I say, it would have been easy. But I think you deserve more than that.

What I have attempted to fashion in this book is a balanced look at hybrids and alternative fuel vehicles. If you are going to make a buying decision based at least partially on the information and opinions contained in this book, information and opinions for which I feel quite personally responsible, I want to make certain they are based on facts, not just conjecture or popular conceptions. And when answers are not irrefutable, you receive the conflicting views that will allow you to make up your own mind.

In some ways it is remarkable to me how politicized the hybrid/ alternative fuel debate has become, because I doubt that anyone out there would raise her or his hand and say, "I want my children to breathe dirty air, drink poisoned water, and be prevented from having the energy sources to make their lives healthy, happy, and prosperous." And I frankly am amazed that many who praise hybrids to the sky, and rightly so, turn their backs on other promising technologies such as the use of homegrown ethanol and high-tech diesel that also can have positive effects on our lives and our environment. After spending months doing research for this book, poring over data, and sorting out conflicting views on the subject, it is my well-considered opinion that all the technologies I describe in this book have their place in what is a grand crusade to make things better. It is my opinion that the world is best served by real, incremental gains arising from the use of many technologies, rather than seeking out one "True Solution."

I have spent the better part of the last quarter century testing, reviewing, writing, and speaking about automobiles. As former editor of *Motor Trend* magazine and now as the executive editorial director of *Kelley Blue Book* and kbb.com as well as the co-host of the radio program "America on the Road," I have had the privilege and responsibility to provide accurate information that can help individuals just like you make good decisions on the purchase of a car, truck, minivan, or SUV. It is a responsibility I take very seriously. And as the father of three young girls, I take the responsibility of advising you on a hybrid or alternative fuel vehicle purchase very seriously as well. It not only affects your family, it also affects mine.

As to the decision of what hybrid or alternative fuel technology you should decide to buy, I will leave it up to you. After revealing to you the facts and informed opinions of many who are experts in fields that include climatology, biology, and anthropology as well as automotive engineering, the choice is yours. The choices aren't easy, and they are more shades of gray than black and white. But I guarantee you this book will be illuminating, and I am confident it will prompt you to think a little more deeply and more rationally about all these important issues. I believe you will make the right decision, and that is important because our lives and our world depend on it.

How to Use This Book

This book has been designed so you can easily access the information you want and need to know right away without hassle. To facilitate that, the book has both a very detailed Table of Contents and a quicker-to-read Contents at a Glance. If you have special areas of interest, feel free to look them up and dive right in.

But if you don't absolutely need to access information on a particular area of interest right away, I encourage you to begin your reading from the beginning, because the book is structured in logical segments that will help you understand the issues better. Chapters 1 and 2 present an overview that puts the hybrid/alternative fuel question in context. They take an incisive look at key issues addressed by the vehicles—issues that go beyond saving money at the gas pump to environmental concerns, global warming, and even world trade and politics. They also look at the history of hybrids and alternative fuels, a look back that has some lessons for us today. Chapters 3 through 9 take a deep dive into the various hybrid and alternative fuel technologies as they exist right now, giving you practical information that includes what it's like to drive, maintain, and refuel the vehicles. And it takes a hard look at the economics of each potential purchase and ownership experience. Finally, Chapters 10 through 12 are about you and the choices you can make. You can decide to keep your current car as is, convert it to some sort of hybrid or alternative fuel vehicle, or purchase another car with the attributes you seek. These chapters help you walk through that maze of decisions. It concludes with a look at the transportation technologies we will see in the future.

No matter how you use this book—as a reference from which you take bits and pieces or a narrative that details the state of hybrids and alt-fuels from the beginning to tomorrow—I trust you will find it useful. And I wish you success in your personal pursuit of the right decision.

Extras

Throughout *The Complete Idiot's Guide to Hybrid and Alternative Fuel Vehicles*, you'll find nuggets of information in bite-size form packaged in what we in the publishing business call sidebars. These sidebars will provide you with good advice that include tips, warnings, and background information. Their purpose is much like spice in cooking—to enrich the experience without overpowering it.

Boosters

This type of sidebar includes tips that can help you get more out of the vehicle you choose.

Potholes _____

These are warnings you should follow when going through the process of finding, buying, and owning the right hybrid or alt-fuel vehicle.

Definitions _____

Some of the terms throughout the book can be unfamiliar to people new to the world of hybrids, so I have included explanations of technical terms and concepts in easy-to-understand form.

Acknowledgments

A book like this takes a great deal of effort from a great many people. I want to thank everyone who offered me an opinion or a bit of advice that I could pass along. There is no doubt that many people are willing to share their opinions about hybrids and alternative fuel vehicles.

This book started with an e-mail from my tireless agent Jake Elwell of Wieser & Elwell, Inc. He had seen the press reports surrounding the latest in a series of gasoline price hikes and believed the time was right for a practical book on hybrids. Knowing my automotive background, he came to me. Over the course of several phone calls I persuaded him that the book should be about more than just hybrids, because other technologies that haven't received the amount of press that hybrids have are also worthy of discussion. He agreed and, quite happily, so did Paul Dinas, senior acquisitions editor at Alpha Books who shepherded my proposal through the approval process. To those men go my personal thanks.

While I am thanking people, I also would like to thank my friends and colleagues at _Kelley Blue Book_, who have been supportive of this effort. Included among them are Paul Johnson, Stephen Henson, Joni Finkle, Jason Allan, Beth Lear, Tiffany Oda, and Robyn Eckard. I'd also like to thank my "America on the Road" radio co-host Mike Anson for his always-sage advice on matters automotive. And the rest of the "America on the Road" crew—Ed Yelin, Al Herskovitz, BJ Killeen, and Micah Muzio—deserve thanks as well. I would be remiss if I failed to thank two men who spurred my book-writing career—Anthony Schneider, who was the brains behind my first title for *The Complete Idiot's Guide* series; and Bob McCord, who was my agent for many years before he left the business and is still a treasured friend.

This book is much better for the work of the Alpha Books development, production, and editing team. My personal thanks to Kayla Dugger, production editor; Tricia Liebig, copy editor; and Ginny Bess Munroe, development editor; for their thoughtful and helpful efforts.

Finally, I would like to thank my wonderful wife Sandi and my terrific children Maddie, Emma, and Greta. Writing a book in the midst of workaday life can put special burdens on an author's family, and all of them came through it with flying colors.

Trademarks

All terms mentioned in this book that are known to be or are suspected of being trademarks or service marks have been appropriately capitalized. Alpha Books and Penguin Group (USA) Inc. cannot attest to the accuracy of this information. Use of a term in this book should not be regarded as affecting the validity of any trademark or service mark.

Chapter 1

Challenges to Our Mobility

In This Chapter

- ◆ Being about more than the price of gas
- ◆ Learning where our oil comes from
- ◆ Sparking a heated debate over global warming
- ◆ Finding how new technology can help

Fuel prices have sent a seismic shock through the finances of tens of millions of Americans. With the current state of the environment, estimates of petroleum reserves and geo-political forces that have triggered a rapid escalation in fuel prices strongly imply that we American car buyers need to change our behavior and look toward more fuel-efficient vehicles. We have to ask, are we willing to use up the remaining fossil fuel on the planet? And perhaps more to the point, if our country lacks petroleum in the quantities we desire, are we willing to do what it takes to secure the supply from foreign sources?

At the same time, concern is growing about the state of our environ-ment and the earth's climate. Many Americans have been worried about issues such as clean air and water for decades, and now concern about those bedrock issues has been extended for fear that we are causing the world's climate to spin out of control. Because we are in a trend of global warming and the emission of carbon dioxide by our vehicles seems to have an effect on this apparent trend, what are we prepared to do to make things right?

So, as you can see, the business of hybrids and alternative fuels is more than a dollars-and-cents issue. When it comes to clean air and water, it cuts right to the bare necessities of life. Although a rapid fuel price hike jump-started interest in the topic, the issues are much more far-reaching than our ability to save $25 a month in gasoline costs. The mainstreaming of hybrids and other fuel-efficient technologies are no longer the domain of the techno-geeks. They are vital to preserving our natural resources and our way of life.

Petroleum: A Scarce Resource

On its face the fossil fuel issue seems a simple one. The logic goes like this: the supply of fossil fuels on Earth is finite; we are using fossil fuels at a prodigious rate, and pretty soon we're going to run out. When you restrict the topic of discussion to petroleum only and disregard other important fossil fuels—coal and natural gas—the basic premise remains the same, but the inferences are even more onerous because there is less petroleum than coal and natural gas. Because you and I need to drive to get to work tomorrow or to take the family on a camping trip, and because we rely on petroleum to allow us to do that, running out is a pretty scary possibility.

But as is so often the case in life, the reality is far more complex than the above-outlined scenario would lead you to believe. Let's look at the premise bit by bit and deconstruct it. First, let's examine the premise that the supply of fossil fuel is finite. That seems to be a given that is commonly accepted, although today's scientific community does not tend to believe that petroleum is derived from the remains of dead dinosaurs, as had long been postulated. The more recent commonly accepted theory is that petroleum is the result of the heating and compression of tiny ancient animals and plants such as zooplankton and

algae. In either case, the conclusion to be drawn is that the earth's supply of petroleum is essentially finite. The question to be asked in light
of the revisionist theory is: if the process continued during thousands of
years of time, do we know that it has stopped or is the earth continuing
to brew up more oil in its bowels somewhere?

Whatever the case, let's agree that fossil fuels, at least as they commonly
exist so that we can use them easily, are a finite resource. As far as we
can determine with utter certainty, no more is being made. Now, certainly there is no doubt we are using them at a prodigious rate, right?

There is no argument there either depending, of course, on what you
consider to be a prodigious rate. The Energy Information Administration, which compiles and publishes the official energy statistics of the
United States government, says the world's population consumes about
84 million barrels of oil per day, or 31 gigabarrels per year. The United
States is the number one oil-consuming nation in the world, largely
because we have the biggest overall economy in the world—we consume almost 21 million barrels of oil a day. Now, by any measure, that's
a lot of oil. It's a lot of oil to find, pump out of the ground, transport by
pipeline and tanker, refine into end products, distribute, and eventually
use to power our transportation. That doesn't even include the other
things it powers, such as this computer I'm typing on right now. When
it comes to gasoline, we in the United States use 384.7 million gallons
a day.

How Much Oil Is There?

Okay, the oil supply is finite and we're using a whole lot of it. Finally,
let's examine the third postulate because that's the really frightening
one—"Pretty soon we're going to run out." That seems to be a commonly held belief. For instance, a Wikipedia.com author says flatly in
his or her discussion of petroleum and petroleum-related issues, "At current consumption levels, world oil supply will be gone in about 33 years."

Now that's the kind of information that will get you up off your couch
ready to do something about it. The problem with statements such as
that is that they are horribly naïve. And this is not to pick on Wikipedia
or those who, with the very best of intentions, beat the drum that our
oil is running low, but it is naïve for several reasons.

> **Boosters** _____
>
> Humankind has been very resourceful in finding new sources of fuel through the eons, yet the shift to fossil fuels has come very recently in human history, beginning in the nineteenth century. There is little reason to believe we can't shift our "fuel of choice" again.

First, nobody knows how much oil there is. Estimates of the total quantity of oil on the planet vary widely, and they are subject to revision. For example, in 1882, the United States Institute of Mining estimated that 95 million barrels of oil remained in the ground. Because production was running at about 25 million barrels a year in those days, it was immediately postulated that we would soon run out. What this didn't take into account was that more oil would be discovered, such as the major Texas discoveries that occurred right after the turn of the century.

This scenario has run its course a dizzying number of times in the last 100 years. It seemed as if in nearly every decade of the previous century there were outcries that we would soon run out of oil. In 1919, the magazine *Scientific American* suggested the United States auto industry couldn't go on ignoring the fact that there were only 20 years' worth of oil left. The following year, in what was the seminal look at overall oil resources, David White, the chief geologist of the U.S. Geological Survey, estimated that the total oil remaining in the United States was 6.7 billion barrels. Today, after 85 years of heavy consumption, oil remaining in the United States is estimated to be between 21.3 and 29.3 billion barrels.

What these estimates and predictions seem to ignore is that we continue to find new sources of petroleum. After the major finds in Texas came the immense discoveries in the Middle East. That was followed by major discoveries of oil in the North Sea and Alaska. And if you think we have found all the oil there is to find, consider the recent discovery of oil made in the depths of the Gulf of Mexico. The 300-square-mile region is estimated to contain between 3 billion and 15 billion barrels of oil and natural gas liquids.

Without trying to take you too deeply into the arcane world of *proven reserves*, *probable reserves*, and *possible reserves*, you should know this: there is more oil on the earth than many take into account when they make their predictions that we will soon run out of oil.

? **Definitions** _____

> **Proven reserves** are oil that the oil industry believes is reasonably certain of being produced using current technology and at current market prices with the acknowledged consent of the governments that may be involved.
>
> **Probable reserves** are oil that the oil industry believes has a reasonable probablity of being produced using current or soon-to-be-developed technology at current market prices, with the involved governments' consent.
>
> **Possible reserves** are oil that the oil industry believes has a chance of being developed under favorable circumstances, and while favorable circumstances can mean many things, in this context it often revolves around the current market price of oil. The higher the price, the more favorable the circumstances.

Many predictions are based on extrapolations of current consumption versus estimates of proven reserves. But as you'll note from its definition, proven reserves is an oil industry term used to define oil by the likelihood of its ability to be extracted profitably from wherever it lodges given current market prices. In other words, if market prices for oil rise, as they have recently done quite dramatically, oil that would not otherwise be economically feasible to produce would become feasible. For instance, deeper drilling and other more expensive extraction techniques would make economic sense given a higher oil price. For this reason alone, proven reserves would increase if the crude oil price increases even if we haven't discovered any more oil. And that doesn't take into account new discoveries, such as what we just experienced in the Gulf of Mexico, which add still more to the proven reserves.

So although it might, at first glance, seem prudent to make predictions of the future based on proven reserves because they are, well, proven, doing so distinctly misrepresents the true picture. There is significantly more oil on Earth that could be available to us than the present estimates of proven reserves would suggest, especially to someone who is unsure of the definition of proven reserves. A reasonable estimate of today's proven reserves is 1,000 gigabarrels (1,000 billion barrels) and a decent estimate of world consumption of oil is 30 to 32 billion barrels a year. If you did the simple math there, you'd arrive at the conclusion that in about 30 years from now we would run out of oil. But as I said, that is naïve.

It is actually naïve in two ways. First, the rate of consumption can be expected to rise during the decades as developing nations use more and more oil, and that would imply we have less than 30 years' worth of oil, but mitigating that trend is the fact that, if this added consumption tends to make oil more expensive as economics says it should, then people will turn to alternative fuels. Hmmm, isn't that what this book is about?

Further, as the price of oil increases, oil that is not now economically viable to produce would become viable and desirable. For instance, the vast tar sands of Venezuela's Orinoco region and the similarly vast tar sands in Canada's Athabasca region could yield petroleum economically giving higher prices for oil.

Before believing the specter of "running out of oil" we need to look at the total picture, not just proven reserves. Experts estimate that the total world resource of oil is somewhere between 2 trillion and 11 trillion barrels. Even the U.S. Geological Survey, which tends to be conservative in its numbers, says that there are 2.2 trillion barrels of recoverable oil on Earth that we know about. Even at our profligate rate of oil consumption these days, this should last us a long time, perhaps well into the twenty-second century.

Where the Oil Is

More important than the potential of "running out of oil" is where we get our oil and the effect that has on the price. Much of the petroleum on which we in the United States rely comes from foreign countries. Each day United States oil wells produce about 5 million barrels of oil, and each day we import 10.1 million barrels. Thus the fate of our transportation system is largely in the hands of foreigners. This conjures up national security issues and is troubling to many people.

That concern is justified, but again, the reality is a bit more complicated than the simplistic rhetoric on the subject would indicate. For one thing, the country from which we import the largest percentage of the petroleum we do import is not some highly insecure Middle Eastern nation but our neighbor to the north, Canada. We also import a substantial amount of crude oil from our neighbor to the south, Mexico.

Of greater concern is the amount of crude oil we import from the *Organization of the Petroleum Exporting Countries (OPEC)*. Some of these countries have unfriendly or unstable governments. It is this instability and potential unfriendliness that really puts our crude oil supply (and thus our gasoline supply) potentially at risk.

How great is that risk? There are several schools of thought on this, but again this risk is not quite as horrendous as it may seem on the surface. For one thing, OPEC countries and other countries from which we buy oil are not a solid bloc. Some are friendly to us, some are much less so. But the important thing to note is that if some countries don't want to sell their oil to us, other countries will quickly move to pick up the slack. No one country, simply by refusing to sell us oil, can cause our oil supply to dry up.

Definitions

The **Organization of the Petroleum Exporting Countries (OPEC)** is an international organization made up of Algeria, Indonesia, Iran, Iraq, Kuwait, Libya, Nigeria, Qatar, Saudi Arabia, the United Arab Emirates, and incongruously, Venezuela.

When you look at the Top 10 countries in terms of proven reserves of oil, you will see a varied picture. The number one and number two countries are Saudi Arabia and Canada, two very different countries no doubt, but both friendly to the United States. Iran, number three on the list, is at this writing very unfriendly to us and Iraq, number four, is largely in chaos. But there are other countries on the list with which we do a substantial amount of trade. Beyond the Top 10 or even the Top 20, as listed on the following page, there are numerous other countries that have substantial amounts of oil. Further, we rank eleventh on the list, and that does not include the recent Gulf of Mexico discoveries, which could double our proven reserves.

Top 20 Oil-Producing Nations

Rank	Country	Proven Reserves (Billion Barrels)
1	Saudi Arabia	264.3
2	Canada	178.8
3	Iran	132.5
4	Iraq	115.0
5	Kuwait	101.5
6	United Arab Emirates	97.8
7	Venezuela	79.7
8	Russia	60.0
9	Libya	39.1
10	Nigeria	35.9
11	United States	29.2
12	China	18.3
13	Qatar	15.2
14	Mexico	12.9
15	Algeria	11.4
16	Brazil	11.2
17	Kazakhstan	9.0
18	Norway	7.7
19	Azerbaijan	7.0
20	India	5.8
N/A	Top 20 countries	90.2
N/A	Rest of world	68.1
N/A	World total	1,292.5

Source: Oil & Gas Journal, Vol. 103, No. 47 (Dec. 19, 2005). (As quoted by the United States Energy Information Administration.)

Although a single country or even a group of countries would have a hard time cutting our oil imports off altogether, what a country or countries could do and, in effect, have done, is substantially raise the price we pay for crude oil and, in turn, substantially raise the price we pay for gasoline at the pump. Unrest and/or threat of war in a region of oil-producing countries quickly sends the world crude oil price rocketing skyward. We have seen this phenomenon occur several times during the last 4 decades with huge "oil shocks" occurring in 1973 to 1974, 1979 to 1980 and, to a somewhat lesser extent, in 2005 to 2006.

These events can be very disruptive, often leading to economic recession. Hundreds of thousands could be thrown out of work as the result of these "economic downturns," and often it is the lowest-income families that take the brunt. This is the key reason—not the fear of running out of oil—that the United States would be well-advised to seek more energy independence from the rest of the world. By gaining such independence, we can prevent our country from being blackmailed by oil-rich foreign countries and we can maintain our way of life and economic prosperity for all citizens without fear that an oil shock will send our progress reeling.

Certainly the proliferation of oil around the globe lessens our risk of economic catastrophe. As an OPEC minister was recently quoted, "It is not that oil is too expensive, it is that it is too cheap." And by too cheap he means both too cheap to be used as an economic cudgel and too cheap to fill the coffers of foreign governments that might be unfriendly to the United States. With that said, United States politicians of both parties agree that our future would be more secure if we could minimize our reliance on foreign oil.

So will we ever run out of crude oil? Experts say it is unlikely because as crude oil grows scarcer in coming years, it will be replaced by other energy sources that are lower-cost. We have seen these transitions before. For most of the centuries before 1800 the predominant fuel was wood. In the mid-1800s wood was supplanted by coal, and in the 1900s petroleum/natural gas took over. There is no reason to believe we cannot make a similar transition to alternative energy sources—ethanol, biodiesel, and hydrogen among them—as the world's economy and lifestyles evolve.

Global Warming

In addition to the threat to our future caused by our reliance on oil, another major threat has reared its ugly head in the last 2 decades. It is the specter of global warming, and it is more than enough to engender fear. Rising sea levels that flood low-lying areas, forest fires, floods, hurricanes, crop failure, disease, pestilence—all these are potential results of unchecked climate change, at least as some tell it. Because most of us find these things to be undesirable, to say the least, all this should be more than enough for us to consider hybrid and alternative fuel vehicles that are expected to mitigate the possible disaster.

The commonly held theory of global warming goes something like this: since the dawn of the Industrial Revolution in the 1800s, human activities such as operating factories, generating stations, and auto-mobiles have led to a startling increase in the amount of carbon dioxide (CO_2) dumped into our atmosphere. This abundance of carbon dioxide (and other greenhouse gases, such as methane) is trapping the sun's heat in the earth's atmosphere as a blanket. That has led to a period of cli-mate change that has been given the convenient handle "global warm-ing." As evidence of this phenomenon researchers point to the fact that 2005 was the hottest year on record and that all 10 of the hottest years recorded have occurred since 1990. This heat, in turn, has already led to natural disasters such as hurricanes and tropical storms and, as evi-dence of that, they cite the fact that there were a record 27 such storms in the Atlantic Ocean in 2005.

But that is nothing compared to what could be coming. First, we are warned to get ready for a significant rise in the sea level, largely because continued warming will cause the melting of glaciers and the polar ice caps. Estimates of this increase in sea level vary, but one highly quoted source predicts a 10- to 11-inch rise in sea level in this century. During the next 5 centuries things are predicted to be much worse—a 20-foot increase in sea level has been predicted. But even sooner than that, a combination of drought, wildfires, and tropical storms brought on by climate change is likely as well.

Okay, that's very scary. Certainly, doing anything we can to mitigate such disasters is worth doing. But in the interest of fairness it is impor-tant to present some actual data on global warming, and a contrarian view on the magnitude of the problem.

Yes, the Earth Has Warmed

Looking at the world's surface temperature records since the dawn of the Industrial Age does reveal an overall warming trend. The increase in surface temperature between 1850 and 2000 was about 1.08 degrees F (0.6 degrees C). Depending on your mindset that may or may not seem cataclysmic, but that doesn't tell the whole story either, because there has not been an uninterrupted increase in global surface temperature.

From 1860 to 1940, records indicate the earth's surface warmed about 0.72 degrees F (0.4 degrees C), but then the earth's surface cooled about 1.8 degrees F (0.1 degrees C) between 1940 and 1980. In fact, some scientists in the 1970s warned of an oncoming Ice Age. From 1980 to 2000, though, the climate reversed itself again and the earth's surface warmed about 0.54 degrees F (0.3 degrees C).

You can make what you will of this data, certainly that's what scientists have done, and what has resulted are conflicting theories on the seriousness of the current trend, if indeed it can be called a trend. But one of the most interesting aspects is that in the period of 1940 to 1980, when the world experienced almost unrestrained industrial expansion and motor vehicles operated without today's exhaust emission controls, the earth's surface actually cooled a bit. Certainly, this data disproves the popular contention in the general media that the earth has been warming steadily for the last 150 years. It simply hasn't.

Looking back at history, scientists have also determined that cycles of cooling and warming have occurred routinely during the course of its millions of years. Although no real scientist disputes the evidence that the earth's surface has indeed increased in temperature (albeit by less than 1.8 degrees F or 1 degree C), little attention is given to the fact that for a period of some 500 years before that the earth was in a phase of general cooling. This period is often referred to as the Little Ice Age, and among its far-reaching effects was the colonization of North America

Boosters

Having some degree of greenhouse effect is a very good thing, because most planets do not and therefore cannot support life as we know it.

by Europeans. That climate change, as well as the other warming and cooling cycles that occurred before it, came well before the Industrial Age and the invention of the automobile.

But that was then and this is now. Because we agree that we are in a period of global warming (and have been for two-plus decades), what has caused it? Many scientists postulate that the major cause is an accumulation of gases in the atmosphere that are having a Greenhouse Effect. In other words, they let the sun's rays in to warm the earth's surface, then trap the heat that might otherwise escape into space.

Identifying the Culprit

Carbon dioxide is generally regarded as the key greenhouse gas culprit in global warming, because there is no doubt that there has been a gigantic increase in atmospheric carbon dioxide since the dawn of the Industrial Revolution. The equally gigantic increase in the world's population has also contributed to this rise in atmospheric CO_2. But, even though carbon dioxide gets the bad rap, water vapor (H_2O) is actually the dominant greenhouse gas. It along with methane, chlorofluorocarbons (CFCs) and other halocarbons, nitrous oxide, and lower-atmosphere ozone all contribute to retaining heat in the atmosphere.

Potholes

Some scientists say the increases in greenhouse gases have had the same effect as burning one 250-watt electric light bulb for every 100 square meters of Earth's surface continuously every second of every day of the year.

Scientists postulate that increases in greenhouse gases have added infrared energy equivalent to increasing the energy transferred to the earth from the sun by 1 percent. They further suggest that for every decade that passes without action to cut the emission rate of greenhouse gases, we're committing the planet to an additional warming of about 0.18 to 0.36 degrees F (0.1 to 0.2 degrees C).

We don't know exactly what effect a temperature increase on that order will bring. Further, we don't know what mitigating effects other natural and man-made occurrences on Earth and in space will have on our climate. What we do know is that, despite the common perception, our climate has never been stable and likely will never be stable. But now, because our actions as humankind do seem to have an effect on climate, it seems prudent to take actions that will help the climate trend toward the status quo rather than pushing in a direction that has uncertain consequences.

Technology Can Bring Efficiency, Flexibility

The good news is that technology can help. Even though we are faced with challenges as never before, the positive answer is that hybrid drive systems, alternative fuels, and even new technology such as "displacement on demand" for conventional vehicles can allow us to drive what we need and want to drive, while still saving significant amounts of fuel and dumping far fewer pollutants and greenhouse gases into our air.

Hybrids Stretch Fuel

Gasoline-electric hybrids have gained special attention in the past year or two because of the many benefits of the technology. Hybrids stretch your fuel dollar by turning in remarkable fuel economy performances, and great fuel economy, in turn, helps us limit our reliance on oil from foreign countries. At the same time hybrids are very clean when it comes to the emission of pollutants, and they are also adept at limiting the output of greenhouse gas carbon dioxide.

Alternative Fuels a Substitute for Oil

In addition to hybrid technology, new fuels are also having the effect of limiting greenhouse gas emissions, conventional pollution, and our reliance of foreign fuel sources. Biodiesel, ethanol, and natural gas all offer benefits in each of these three important areas in comparison to gasoline. That is why they are gaining in popularity with every passing minute.

New Internal Combustion Vehicles More Efficient

Just as fuels are evolving, so are internal combustion engines. In the gasoline engine's more than 100 years of history it has continually evolved to the point where the best of today's engines are able to emit just miniscule amounts of pollution. New technology is also allowing large gasoline engines to achieve fuel economy more synonymous with smaller engines by shutting down individual cylinders when they are not needed. On the diesel side, the new clean diesel technology along with low-sulfur fuels has resulted in diesel engines that are just as clean as their gasoline counterparts but significantly more fuel-efficient.

New Electrics

Finally, advancing technology is prompting another look at electric cars. Wind- and solar-generated power is becoming more efficient, while many are taking a second look at nuclear reactors as a possible source of cheap power. Pure electric vehicles are waiting for a breakthrough in battery technology to improve their viability, and even though we haven't got there yet, new developments in battery tech are promising, as long as this laptop doesn't catch on fire!

Though we don't have all the answers to the vexing issues of oil supply, global climate change, and the effects of humankind's efforts on Mother Earth, we do know many of the questions. And from those questions, answers to your own individual questions will grow.

The Least You Need to Know

- A sharp jump in fuel prices has spurred consumers to look at hybrid and alternative fuel vehicles, but issues such as the depletion of our fossil fuels and global warming offer additional reasons to investigate these new types of vehicles.

- The world's oil supply is essentially finite but, contrary to what doomsayers tell you, that does not mean we are running out of oil. Who owns the oil, not how much there is, is the real issue.

- There is more debate about global warming than is generally known. The world's climate has never been stable, so periods of heating and cooling are "normal," but it is prudent to limit the production of greenhouse gases such as carbon dioxide when we can.

- In addressing critical issues such as the depletion of fossil fuels and global warning, the good news is that there are high-tech solutions, including hybrids and alternative fuel vehicles.

2

Brief History of Alternative Propulsion Technology

In This Chapter

- ◆ Pulling alternative fuel out of the closet
- ◆ Taking the steam out of steam
- ◆ Looking back at electric cars, circa 1900
- ◆ Spinning wheels got to go 'round

Just a few months ago, gasoline-electric, hybrid-powered cars were anchored firmly on the outer fringes of the automobile marketplace. And that position was far better than the one in which they dwelled a decade ago, because then one could say they were not precisely in the auto marketplace at all. The handful of hybrid vehicles that were on the road were hand-built by a somewhat unruly collection of backyard tinkerers, leftfield electrical engineers, and obscure corporate skunkworks.

Although not quite the sole domain of yurt-dwelling Oregonians or geeky *Popular Mechanics* subscribers, cars that ran on anything but good old gasoline were long considered a bit suspect. Not just a niche, they were pictured by many to be downright weird. After all, hybrids are the antithesis of the vehicle that has ruled the road during the last 15 years—the gas-guzzling SUV, shamelessly burning precious gasoline at a rate of a dozen miles per gallon. But hybrids and alternative fuels have actually been around for decades. It simply has taken a big fuel price jump, rising environmental consciousness, and computer technology to bring them to the fore.

One thing to keep in mind is that there was a time when gasoline cars represented alternative fuel technology. There was a time when building a practical gasoline engine seemed to be a gigantic technical challenge and harnessing it for use in an automotive conveyance seemed so horribly difficult it appeared that there were much better solutions, such as steam and electricity, to providing personal mobility. There was a time when those were mainstream, and gasoline was on the oddball edge.

Steam Cars

It is not difficult to see why late nineteenth century inventors gravitated to steam power when they began to play with the idea of replacing the horse as the motive power for the carriage. By that time steam engines were powering factories that heralded prosperity by belching out thick clouds of black smoke. And steam engines were also propelling the railroad trains that put newly manufactured goods from those factories into willing consumers' hands.

By 1889, when Carl Benz and Gottleib Daimler individually put together what many consider the first automobiles, steam had been powering vehicles for decades. In fact, the idea for a steam-powered car dates back all the way to 1665 when a Flemish Jesuit priest named Ferdinand Verbiest drew up plans for a small steam-powered carriage for Chinese Emperor Khang Hsi. There is no record that the car was ever built, but 100 years later a French artillery officer, Nicolas Josef Cugnot, persuaded his superiors to fund his attempt to build a practical steam-powered vehicle for hauling cannons and cannonballs. Moving forward in fits-and-starts, both literally and figuratively, the convey-ance did make its lumbering way through the streets of the French countryside, but its limited range (a theme we shall see repeated over and over) meant it wasn't very practical. After Cugnot had the first recorded automobile crash in his invention, the French funding dried up, and Cugnot lapsed back into obscurity.

Fast (if you will pardon the expression) forward another 75 years, and you'll find that steam had become a reasonably reliable method of employing power. By that time James Watt and Richard Trevithick had developed high-pressure steam engines installed in locomotives that could pull strings of cars along railways, and Robert Fulton had installed a steam engine in a riverboat. What remained was to use a steam engine in a vehicle that was compact and maneuverable enough to travel the rudimentary roads of the day. That occurred in Britain in 1825 when Goldsworthy Gurney built a steam-powered carriage (later shortened to "car") that not only ran, but was practical enough to com-plete an 85-mile trip in just 10 hours.

By the time twin brothers Francis Edgar and Freelan O. Stanley sold their photographic equipment business in 1897 to go into the business of building motorcars, steam was so well-established that it seemed a no-brainer compared to the continued difficulties tinkerers were having with infant gasoline engines. The brothers sold the rights to their first steam car to the Locomobile Company, which then began to produce them in reasonably large numbers. By 1900, steam was the predomi-nant powerplant under American car hoods. That year United States car manufacturers built 1,681 steam cars, 1,575 electric cars, and just 936 gasoline cars. In a poll conducted at the first National Automobile Show in New York City that year, patrons favored electric-ity as their first choice, followed closely by steam. After seeing how big their idea was get-ting, the Stanleys jumped back into the car business in 1902, establishing the Stanley Motor Carriage Company. They suc-cessfully sold steam cars until about 1920.

> **Boosters**
>
> Using steam, the Stanley brothers set a world land speed record of 127.7 miles per hour during a run at Daytona Beach in 1906. The Stanleys were awarded the prestigious Dewar Trophy for automotive excellence.

There were many reasons to recommend steam as an engine type for early cars. The technology is relatively simple. Water is heated to the boiling point in a closed container (called unimaginatively the "boiler") making steam, and because it is contained within the boiler, the pressure grows as more and more water vaporizes. The high-pressure steam is then directed into a cylinder where it pushes a piston, which, through a linkage, turns a shaft. This shaft, in turn, drives the wheels. One of the several beauties of a steam engine is that it generates a large portion of its power even at very low engine revolutions (the literal rotations of the shaft). This means that, unlike a gasoline-powered car that requires a clutch and series of gears to successfully use the narrow band of power produced by the engine, a steam car channels its power directly to the driving wheels. Add more steam, and you go faster. Lessen the amount of steam going into the engine, and you go slower. Simple. Effective.

> **Boosters**
>
> Because of its awesome off-the-line power potential, a steam car would make a great drag racing vehicle. Sadly, drag racing came along too late for steamers to show their goods.

The Stanley Brothers extolled the virtues of the direct-drive system and touted steam versus what they referred to as the "internal explosion engine," their term for the internal combustion gasoline engine. At first, their cars also used gasoline as fuel, burning it in a simple "firebox" under the boiler, while later steamers used kerosene. Though their advertising alluded to the dangers of the gasoline engine, the big fear that revolved around a steam car was a boiler explosion. Safety valves that vented dangerous pressure were the simple answer to that potential danger, but the threat was more real than imagined.

So why don't we drive steam cars today? Well, steamers have two major flaws. They take a long time to "start" and they have (you will hear this tune again) limited range. As to the first problem, the Stanleys and others couldn't get past the complication that before a steam car could move it had to, literally, get steam up. In other words, water in the boiler had to be heated like water in a tea kettle until there was enough accumulated steam to begin driving the pistons. This usually took several minutes, so a steamer was a terrible choice as a robber's getaway car.

The other issue is range. Because they needed steam to move, steam cars required water, and when the water ran out, they were stranded until more water could be added. Later, steamers addressed this issue with "condensers" that would turn the steam back into water, so it could be reused. But steam cars never entirely got past the need for adding water, which limited their range.

In contrast, inventors quickly solved many of the problems associated with gasoline-powered cars, most important among them the necessity to crank-start the engine. With the advent of the self-starter, steam cars' days were numbered, and by 1920, they were, effectively, museum pieces. Private aviation pioneer Bill Lear tried to revive steam cars in the 1960s and 1970s, but his concepts never got past the prototype stages.

Electric Cars, Round One

Those automotive pioneers who didn't gravitate toward steam power found electricity an appealing alternative. After Benjamin Franklin's research into the properties of electricity in the eighteenth century, progress in the field moved forward very rapidly with the discovery of galvanic cells by Luigi Galvani around 1786. Count Alessandro Giuseppe Antonio Anastasio Volta moved that research still further, and he is often credited with the invention of the electric battery. By 1835, experiments conducted by John Frederic Daniell and Michael Faraday had resulted in much improved batteries and rudimentary electric motors that could be powered by them.

Drawing on the progress being made, in 1839, Scotsman Robert Anderson built what is generally regarded to be the first electric vehicle. Unfortunately for Anderson (and our air quality), battery technology at the time had not advanced to the point of creating a rechargeable battery. The batteries in Anderson's car had to be replaced when they

Boosters

Batteries create electricity by putting two dissimilar materials into a solution that conducts electricity. Because of a phenomenon known as electrolysis, electrons flow from one material to the other. This flow of electrons is electricity.

were exhausted, meaning the car was impractical for everyday use. It wasn't until the 1860s when Raymond Gaston Plante invented the lead-acid battery that a reliable, rechargeable battery reached common use, and it took further developments by Emile Alphonse Faure to make those batteries suitable for motor vehicles. After that, though, the dam of innovation burst.

Even though Sir David Salomon's 1870 attempt to build a practical electric car was doomed by the weight and poor storage capacity of its batteries, by 1886, battery technology had improved to the point that electric taxicabs were in use in England, and Jack the Ripper may well have taken one to escape one of his grisly murder scenes. Two years later, Immisch & Company built a four-passenger carriage, powered by a one-horsepower motor and 24-cell battery, for the Sultan of the Ottoman Empire. Meanwhile Magnus Volk of Brighton, England, constructed and tested a three-wheeled electric car.

By the late 1890s, electric vehicles were becoming fairly common, at least in a few large cities. New York boasted a modern fleet of electric cabs, and in London, Walter Bersey designed a taxi for the London Electric Cab Company that featured a three-horsepower electric motor with a range of 50 miles between charges.

Although use of taxis in large urban areas spoke to electric vehicles' major strengths—reliable, silent transport at moderate speeds for short trips—entrepreneurs couldn't help seeing a consumer market for electric vehicles. The Pope Manufacturing Company of Hartford, Connecticut, was the leading light of this trend in the United States. By 1899, it had merged its operations with two other electric car manufacturers, changing its name to the Electric Vehicle Company. Its production numbers rivaled that of Oldsmobile and the Duryea brothers, who were building gasoline-powered cars. In Europe, a name that would become synonymous with performance cars cut his eyeteeth on an electric vehicle. Dr. Ferdinand Porsche's first design was the Lohner Electric Chaise.

Because cross-country journeys by car in those days took on many aspects of an expedition due to the rudimentary nature of inter-city roads, electric vehicles thrived through the first decade-and-a-half of the twentieth century. Woods, Detroit Electric, Waverly, and Baker were all successfully building and marketing electric cars. With closed bodies to keep out chill winds and a simple driving procedure, the electrics were perfect for around-town use, and they were the first choice of female drivers of the era. The fact that they were quiet and didn't belch noxious smoke also gained them adherents.

There also was something sublime about their operation. Using the properties of electromagnetism, electric motors could be very compact, yet very powerful. Because they have relatively few moving parts, they are inherently durable as well. The final bonus is that many of them can, when operated "in reverse," generate electricity, so the kinetic motion of a coasting electric vehicle can be used to charge its storage batteries.

But the batteries! Ah, that was the rub. As a medium of energy storage their performance was (and remains) so-so at best. Throughout their history the problem surrounding batteries has been the same: their worst feature is their weight and mass. They are heavy for the amount of energy they can store, and that issue eventually proved to be the downfall of the electric car.

> **Potholes**
>
> Who killed the electric car? It was not a "who" but a "what," namely its batteries. Up until today, battery technology has prevented us from enjoying practical electric vehicles.

It was an issue, by the way, that was recognized very early. Dr. Porsche's second vehicle design attempted to deal with the shortcomings of battery storage. It was a hybrid vehicle that used an internal combustion engine to power a generator that, in turn, sent current to electric motors in the wheel hubs. The good doctor was not alone. The automotive history of the first decade of the twentieth century is littered with hybrid vehicles that tried to use gasoline and electricity to supplement one another. The Woods Motor Vehicle Company of Chicago had an even stranger method of dealing with the shortcomings of electric vehicle technology. Its Interurban model of 1905 allowed the owner to swap its electric powertrain for a two-cylinder gasoline engine when longer vehicle range was desired. The company claimed this transplant could be done in less than an hour's time, but very few buyers took them up on it.

By 1910, overland vehicle durability runs were all the rage, sending electric cars on their way to oblivion. The deathblow came with the invention of the self-starter for the gasoline engine. By eliminating the onerous chore of turning a crank to start the engine, gasoline cars suddenly gained much greater appeal. By the time the self-starter arrived, pioneers such as Ransom Olds, David Dunbar Buick, and Henry Ford had their factories churning out thousands of reasonably affordable gasoline cars, and the cheap, reliable self-starter was icing on the cake. Electric cars wouldn't resurface on the vehicle radar screen until the 1960s.

Turbine Cars

When I was a young pup immersing myself in the technologies that would certainly propel our cars of the future, electrics, hybrids, natural gas cars, or alternative fuel vehicles didn't even reach my consciousness. In the mid-1960s, it was obvious to anyone who was following the pulse of technological change that by 1980, all our cars would be powered by gas turbines. Turbines were *it*. High-tech, powerful, and compact, turbines were simply the obvious choice for replacing the conventional gasoline engine. And one thing is obvious in all this—throughout the decades somebody somewhere has *always* wanted to replace the gasoline engine.

There is a simple elegance to the gas turbine concept that is appealing both from an engineering and from an aesthetic sense. On a basic level, a gas turbine is a rotary-type engine that extracts force from the burning of an air-fuel mixture in a combustion chamber by using the expanding gases to spin the turbine's blades. The spinning shaft at the hub of the rotating blades can be used to drive a car's wheels, a ship's propeller, or a helicopter's rotor. A turbine is closely related to a jet engine, but although a jet uses the expansion of the fuel-air mixture burning within it to provide thrust, the turbine captures the force of that burning, expanding air-fuel mix via its spinning blades.

> **Boosters**
>
> Turbine engines have gained popularity in light aircraft. In so-called "turboprops," propellers are connected to the spinning rotor shaft, pulling the plane through the air.

On the ground, British car manufacturer Rover introduced its Jet1 gas-turbine-powered concept car in 1950. Designed by a team led by F. R. Bell and engineered under the direction of technical whiz Maurice Wilks, the two-seat rear, mid-engine sportster could reach speeds of 78 miles per hour running on gasoline, paraffin, or diesel fuel. As with diesel, a turbine can burn a wide variety of flammable liquids.

On this side of the Atlantic, Chrysler took up the turbine mantle. The company experimented with turbines throughout the 1950s and by 1963 it was prepared to put 50 of them into consumers' hands for a long-term test. Though the bodies were built by Ghia in Italy, the cars had styling similar to conventional Chrysler products of the day. Under the hood, however, was an extremely radical fourth-generation Chrysler turbo engine, which ran at engine speeds of about 45,700 rpm. In comparison, a conventional gasoline engine's crankshaft turns at a maximum of about 7,500 rpm.

Similar to the Rover engine, the Chrysler turbo didn't really care what it drank, running on kerosene, jet fuel, unleaded gasoline, or even vegetable oil. Its power shaft was connected to a conventional Chrysler-built automatic transmission. Twin rotating regenerators, which transferred exhaust heat to the inlet air, greatly improved fuel economy, but even so the Chrysler turbine cars were horrendously thirsty. Poor throttle response and tepid acceleration also dogged the car, and the crowning blow was its sound—rather than the manly rumble of a big American V-8 engine, it sounded like the suck of a powerful vacuum cleaner.

Though the Chrysler turbine-car test was a flop, turbine adherents weren't about to throw in the rotor. The turbine engine concept got a big boost in 1967 when famed driver Parnelli Jones came within a whisker of winning the Indianapolis 500 in a turbine-powered race car. Only the failure of a cheap, non-turbine-related part prevented Jones from bagging the big prize. The turbine returned the following year with Joe Leonard at the wheel of a wedge-shaped Lotus and again dominated the race before another nonturbine failure cost him the win eight laps from victory. After that the race sanctioning body outlawed turbines altogether, a sure sign that the technology was good.

But as practical automotive powerplants for the average person, turbines aren't practical. Though small and light, they are not as immediately responsive to the accelerator pedal as are gasoline cars. Even race car drivers noted this tendency. In addition, they are expensive to build; run at very high rpm, which can engender maintenance issues; and worst of all, they are not very adept at dealing with varied loads—just the kinds of loads that car engines must accommodate. For example, 65 mph cruising, bumper-to-bumper traffic, stops and starts around town, and full-throttle acceleration for passing.

General Motors thought the turbine engine might be a good answer for a hybrid powerplant. In a hybrid the engine could run within narrow ranges because it only was designed to supply power for the battery pack. But the hybrid EV1 with the turbine was not a success, and these days no one is talking about turbines as a serious replacement for the conventional piston engine.

Hybrids—Before the Japanese

Although the common perception is that Toyota and Honda invented hybrid vehicles less than 10 years ago, nothing could be further from the truth. We simply don't know who invented the first hybrid car, because experiments in hybrid technology go back to the beginning of automobile history. As we've noted, gasoline "spark" engines have their idiosyncrasies and electric motors and their associated batteries don't present a perfect solution either, so inventors quickly tried to combine the two in an effort to offset their weaknesses.

As early as 1900, two hybrid cars were displayed at the Paris Auto Salon, the precursor of the Paris Auto Show. Several companies that built taxicabs decided they could add range to their electric propulsion systems if they added a small gasoline engine to keep the batteries charged. Krieger, Pieper, and Auto-Mixte were three of the companies that built hybrids between 1900 and 1910. The Pieper car was especially interesting, because it used the gasoline engine to charge the batteries and to power the driving wheels, but when an added boost was needed, it used the electric motor to provide supplemental power. The motor also was used to generate electricity for the batteries when the car was in cruising mode.

Hybrids weren't confined to just cabs and other light cars either. Auto-Mixte and Commercial built trucks using hybrid techniques. The Auto-Mixte system was very similar to that used by Pieper, but Commercial, a Philadelphia-based company, took a different course. It used a large multicylinder engine to generate electricity that it sent directly to electric motors to drive the wheels. This eliminated the need for a transmission and a battery pack.

After the advent of the self-starter, most auto engineers turned away from hybrid concepts, although you could make the case that a gasoline-engine car with an electric-powered self-starter *is* a hybrid. In fact, one of the newest hybrids on the market uses the starter motor as a generator and a supplemental power supply to the gasoline engine during hard acceleration. For more information, see Chapter 12.

Woods and Baker tried to buck the rising tide of gasoline by offering gasoline-electric hybrids, but the cost was through the roof, and few purchased the cars. Among the last gasps of the early hybrids was the Owens Magnetic, an otherwise conventional-looking car of 1921, which used a hybrid system similar to commercial trucks. Its gasoline engine powered a generator that, in turn, sent electricity to wheel-mounted motors. In essence, it used the hybrid system to replace the bulky manual transmissions of the era, but it failed to catch on.

After that it would be nearly 50 years before hybrids again gained much attention, and when that attention came it wasn't from the Japanese but from American car companies. Spurred by Clean Air legislation, General Motors began playing with hybrid concepts in the 1960s, and by the end of the decade it had built a two-cylinder gasoline-electric hybrid that could travel at 40 mph.

The Arab Oil Embargo spurred further research into the hybrid concept. Among the most notable: Volkswagen built and submitted a vehicle it called the "Taxi" for Department of Energy testing. Able to switch between electric and gasoline engine power, it eventually recorded 8,000 road miles and became an auto show curiosity. Even more notable was the attempt by engineer-entrepreneurs Victor Wouk and Charles Rosen to qualify their company, Petro-Electric Motors, for financial support under provisions of the Federal Clean Car Incentive Program. Using a Buick Skylark as the basis of their hybrid car, the vehicle reportedly passed all the Environmental Protection Agency tests but the company didn't receive federal support.

That didn't mean that hybrids weren't on the United States government agenda, however. In the mid-1970s, the U.S. Energy Research and Development Administration began a government program to advance hybrid technology, and Congress enacted the Electric and Hybrid Vehicle Research, Development, and Demonstration Act. A decade later, German automaker Audi pulled the wraps off its Audi Duo hybrid, which used a 13-horsepower electric motor to drive the rear wheels while a 123-horsepower 2.3-liter gasoline engine drove the front wheels.

This helped prompt the Clinton Administration to create a new federal initiative called the Partnership for a New Generation of Vehicles (PNGV). A consortium of the government and the American auto industry, the PNGV had the goal of developing an extremely low-pollution car that also could record 80 miles-per-gallon fuel economy. As the years progressed, it became more and more apparent to those working on the program that a hybrid vehicle was the only way to achieve the goal. After the expenditure of more than a billion dollars, three hybrid prototypes eventually emerged from the program. None of them went into production.

The exclusion of Honda and Toyota from the American program prompted those companies to step up their research on hybrid vehicles. Toyota created a project called Global Car for the Twenty-First Century, which eventually spawned the first Toyota Prius hybrid. After Toyota pulled its timetable ahead significantly, the Prius went on sale in Japan in 1997, just prior to the now-famous Kyoto conference on global warming. That same year Audi began to produce its Audi Duo hybrid for public sale. It used a 1.9-liter turbo-diesel engine teamed with a 29 horsepower electric motor powered by lead-acid gel-cell batteries, but it flopped in Europe, and Europeans have been slow to warm to the hybrid concept since.

Boosters

Toyota pushed up the production date of the first Prius hybrid car by some two years so it could take advantage of the publicity surrounding the pivotal Kyoto conference on global warming.

By the late 1990s, American manufacturers had moved their concentration away from hybrids and toward pure electrics, because they knew that hybrids could not achieve the zero-emissions performance required by the California Air Resources Board zero-emissions mandate. In this era, General Motors introduced its famed EV1 to the public, while other companies took a somewhat lower profile with their electrics designed to meet the California standard.

Meanwhile Honda beat Toyota to the punch of introducing the first modern hybrid to the American market when it unveiled the two-seat Honda Insight in 1999. The car offered startling Environmental Protection Agency mileage ratings, and it was quickly followed by an American version of the Toyota Prius.

Initially the hybrids were viewed more as curiosities than as a solution, especially because they failed to meet the California zero-emissions mandate. But when that mandate was rescinded and pure electrics disappeared, hybrids became the best bet for those seeking high fuel economy with strong environmental benefits.

The Least You Need to Know

- ◆ Alternative technology dates back to the beginnings of the automobile, because the gasoline engine has always been a cantankerous assemblage of parts and pieces.

- ◆ The first cars were powered by steam, and steam power offered several advantages versus gasoline, but it had a fatal flaw—range.

- ◆ Although electric cars seem new and high tech, they date back to the 1830s. In comparison to gasoline vehicles, they too have a fatal flaw—battery technology.

- ◆ American car manufacturers in combination with the United States government have pursued turbine and hybrid vehicles since the 1950s, but it took Japanese manufacturers to introduce hybrids to the American buying public.

3

Green for Sale Today

In This Chapter

- ◆ Hitting the big time with alternative fuels
- ◆ Witnessing the quiet revolution in diesel
- ◆ Looking to an atomic power future?
- ◆ Discovering what the car of the future might be

Gasoline-electric hybrids have, up until now, stolen the show when it comes to fuel efficiency, but there are other technologies that are worthy of attention. In addition to gasoline-electric hybrid vehicles, epitomized by the ubiquitous Toyota Prius, another alternative fuel technology available in dealer showrooms today is flexible fuel, or Flex Fuel, vehicles that can use a gasoline-ethanol mix. In fact, Flex Fuel vehicles far outnumber hybrids on today's roads. The only problem is many of them are currently using gasoline for fuel. In addition, clean diesel and natural gas-powered vehicles, while now even rarer than hybrids, are expected to gain in popularity. Despite being maligned by many, the gasoline engine is constantly being refined and improved. For example, some of the newest gasoline engines use computer technology to optimize fuel economy by shutting down cylinders when their power is not needed. Finally, for short hops and urban situations electric cars have a place, and a breakthrough in battery technology and a revival in the use of nuclear power generation could push electric cars back into the prominence they enjoyed in 1900.

There is no doubt that hybrids and alternative fuel vehicles are rocketing skyward in popularity. According to research by R. L. Polk & Company, which tallies U.S. vehicle registrations, there are now 9 million such vehicles on U.S. roads. Lest you think that this is a very recent phenomenon, some 8.3 million of those vehicles were on the road by the end of 2005, and 700,000 more hybrid, diesel, and ethanol vehicles were purchased in 2006. The Alliance of Automobile Manufacturers, an industry organization, is ambitiously predicting that its member companies will sell 2 million hybrid/alternative fuel vehicles in 2008. Because there were only 3 million alternative fuel vehicles and hybrids on U.S. roads in 2000, the growth has been remarkable.

> **Boosters**
>
> At the end of 2006, about 50 separate Flex Fuel, hybrid, natural gas, and clean diesel models were available for sale in the United States. A similar number are currently in development.

Although hybrids get most of the ink, Flex Fuel vehicles get the bulk of the sales. Compared with the overall United States auto market, hybrid sales still are small. Automakers sold about 266,000 hybrids in the United States in 2006, making them about 1.6 percent of the overall market, according to J.D. Power and Associates. By 2013, the research firm estimates that the number will grow to 900,000 hybrids or around 5 percent of the overall market. Other experts say that prediction is too rosy.

One facet of the hybrid market that is not well understood is how regional it is. On a year-over-year basis, hybrid registrations were up 35 percent in 2006 versus 2005, but most of the gains came in the state of California. The Golden State represents 13 percent of the total United States light vehicle market, but it accounts for more than 25 percent of United States hybrid sales. In fact, more than 12 percent of hybrid sales took place in the Los Angeles area alone. American trends frequently begin in California, so that might speak well for the future of hybrids. But if the trend to hybrids is simply driven by the desire to commute in the carpool lane, the future won't be so promising.

One thing is sure: if hybrids don't find a future in the United States, they are unlikely to find a future anywhere. Around 70 percent of the some 300,000 hybrid vehicles sold worldwide go to buyers in the United States. Japan, the supposed hotbed of hybrids, buys just 21 percent of the hybrid vehicles purchased each year, and western Europe, despite its highly visible "Green" movement, buys just 8 percent.

 Potholes

Highly populous Asian countries, including China and India, are filled with consumers who want to own their first cars. If they don't embrace hybrids and alternative fuels, it could have a very negative effect on our global air quality.

Even though hybrids are the darlings of the media and the Hollywood community, they have yet to catch on with more than the fringes of the general public. J.D. Power and Associates predict that their market share will more than double in less than a decade, but even then the prospect is that hybrids will be relatively low-sales adjuncts to much more popular conventional models such as Toyota Camry, Honda Accord, and Chevrolet Tahoe. (A progressive two-mode Tahoe hybrid will be introduced in the 2008 model year.) And those low sales could threaten the future of hybrids altogether, because auto companies like building relatively few models in large quantities.

The Clean Diesel Revolution

Although hybrids have been stealing the limelight, a quiet revolution in fuel technology has been occurring, largely unnoticed. It is the shift to low-sulfur diesel fuel, a shift that will make the epitome of clean diesel technology available here in the United States.

The new diesel contains just 3 percent of the pollution-generating and filter-clogging sulfur of that in the previous diesel blend sold in the United States. (Europe has been running on low-sulfur diesel for several years now.) The fuel mixture has two key benefits.

Potholes

The rotten egg smell attributed to sulfur is really the unappealing odor of hydrogen sulfide. However, sulfur in the atmosphere does stink, because it is a major contributor to acid rain.

It severely limits the amount of sulfur expelled into the air from diesel engines. That's good because sulfur is bad. Even more importantly, it will open the way to the spread of clean diesel technology in America's cars and trucks, progress that was blocked by the previous fuel's sulfur content.

The difference in our air quality and in oil reliance on foreign fuels should be substantial. Diesel engines are significantly more efficient than gasoline engines, but their progress in the United States was stymied because of stringent pollution standards that could not be met by then-current diesel technology. As you probably could guess, diesels of the past were not pretty. How bad were they? In 1995, gasoline-powered cars outnumbered diesel-powered trucks and buses by 28 to 1, yet diesel vehicles emitted 43 percent of the smog-forming nitrogen oxides and more than two thirds of the soot particles that went into our air. Although the move to low-sulfur diesel fuel will have its most immediate effects by helping clean up the pollution emitted by big trucks and buses, it also is expected to result in a substantial increase in high-fuel-mileage diesel cars and SUVs.

Surprise! Nuclear Might Return

Our dependence on foreign sources of energy has been well-documented. Review Chapter 1 for this evidence. Hybrids and alternative fuel vehicles are methods by which we can limit or even end this dependence, but many hybrid advocates have avoided talking up a source of energy that, on the face of it, could play a huge part in putting our nation's energy future in our own hands—atomic power.

The economic appeal is obvious. Atomic power is a very cheap way to generate electricity, and electricity is a very cheap way to power cars. Look at it this way: with gasoline at $2.50 a gallon, you will pay 12.5¢ a mile if your car averages 20 miles per gallon. But at the national average retail price for electricity, a car that goes 4 miles on a kilowatt-hour would cost just more than 2 cents a mile to run. And because nuclear power can be cheaper than other methods of generating electricity, most of which require fossil fuels, the cost of driving an electric car recharged from a nuclear power grid likely would be even less.

Since the Three Mile Island nuclear accident occurred in 1979, no new nuclear electric generating plants have been built in the United States. No one was killed in that near-catastrophe, but the same cannot be said about the disaster that unfolded at Chernobyl in the then-Soviet Union seven years later. Those two disturbing events proved enough to halt United States construction of atomic power facilities, especially because even prior to the two accidents a strong anti-nuclear movement existed here in America.

But the ban on new facilities has not stopped U.S. nuclear power altogether. In fact, in facilities that were in place by 1979, nuclear energy production has actually expanded three-fold. In 2005, the 103 U.S. commercial nuclear reactors operating in 31 states generated 782 billion kilowatt-hours (kWh). At the same time, other countries have been far less reticent to add atomic power-generating plants than we have. Today, more than 300 nuclear reactors produce electricity in some 30 countries, and another 125 or so are under construction worldwide.

The power that can be unleashed by nuclear fission is nearly miraculous and, at the same time, can be monstrous in the case of a runaway nuclear accident or, worse yet, a nuclear explosion. But of all the energy sources in wide use around the world, nuclear fission has no peer for efficiency. A gram of uranium 235 contains as much energy potential as 4 tons of coal.

> **Boosters** _____
>
> Pound for pound, coal stores twice as much energy as wood, and oil stores twice as much energy as coal. But a gram of uranium 235 is nearly off the charts when compared to these three conventional energy sources.

Public opinion in the United States seems to be shifting in favor of nuclear power, spurred by recent crude oil, natural gas, and gasoline price hikes. But reviving America's nuclear future is hardly a done deal. Interestingly, some who are vociferous advocates of hybrid and electric vehicles are equally vociferous opponents of the expansion of nuclear power. Certainly there are legitimate questions to be answered about nuclear power plant safety and equally legitimate questions to be answered about the disposal of spent nuclear fuel. It is that second issue that is currently the hobgoblin that is preventing nuclear power from going forward. But if that issue is solved, nuclear power could enjoy a flowering like it has never seen before, and electric cars would enjoy a strong renaissance.

Even lacking a battery advancement that would drastically increase the range of electric cars and trucks, the proliferation of cheap electric power could spur the development of a "smart electric grid." Today if you plug in your vehicle at your neighbor's house or your employer's office, you don't pay for that electricity. But in a "smart grid" the power generating a supply system recognizes the electric vehicle as yours wherever you plug it in and will bill you accordingly. This should make routine recharging, even in the middle of the day, much more convenient, increasing the usefulness of electric vehicles markedly.

A Peek at the Future

In Chapter 2, I floated the idea that today's conventional gasoline-powered cars are, in reality, a mild type of hybrid vehicle. They use their gasoline engines to move themselves, but other functions, such as powering audio and navigation systems, heating and ventilating fans and the crucial electronic engine control and ignition systems are powered by a storage battery that is kept in a proper state of charge by the gasoline engine. Even starting the gasoline engine is accomplished by the use of an electric motor, again powered by the battery. Given that this is now considered "conventional," it is not too difficult to imagine a day when a variety of separate systems now considered exotic or "alternative" could merge within a vehicle and become the new convention.

To make that vision more concrete, imagine a vehicle with a displacement on demand, turbocharged, internal combustion engine fueled by a biofuel (biodiesel or ethanol) whose starter motor also acts as a torque-booster for quick acceleration and as a generator to keep the high-capacity battery bank charged. Imagine further that this engine has very advanced catalytic converters and particulate filtering, a fuel system that eliminates evaporative emissions and that the accessories and ancillaries are powered by the battery rather than by engine power. A second electric motor incorporated within the transmission is available to supplement the internal combustion engine and starter/generator motor when peak acceleration is needed. The vehicle also would feature auto-stop start for its engine and utilize regenerative braking/coasting to keep its battery bank charged.

This is not such a stretch because the Saab BioPower Hybrid concept vehicle has many of these attributes. Unveiled in 2006, the innovative vehicle lacks a displacement on demand engine, largely because its 2.0-liter turbocharged engine is already rather small, but it has virtually all the other attributes of our mythical future vehicle.

Saab's modular hybrid system features a maintenance-free, 300-volt battery bank, a 38-kilowatt (kW) rear-mounted electric motor, a 15-kW integrated starter generator, and an all-wheel-drive via electric power transmission to the rear wheels. As sophisticated as it is, the entire hybrid system is housed within an otherwise standard Saab 9-3 Convertible without sacrificing interior accommodations or trunk space.

The all-aluminum 2.0-liter BioPower engine is modified to run on pure E100 bioethanol fuel and operates in tandem with the electrical power system. This offers fuel-saving stop/start functionality, torque-boosting electric power assistance on demand, regenerative braking, and an electric-only "Zero Mode" for city driving. Saab touts the vehicle as giving "zero fossil CO_2 exhaust emissions," but that is a bit disingenuous because it does create CO_2 emissions; they are simply from the burning of biofuel, not fossil fuel.

The engine incorporates an integrated starter generator (ISG) and also charges a substantial battery bank mounted under the floor of the trunk. The compact 42-volt ISG, built into the flywheel between the engine and transmission, is the key to the car's fuel-saving stop/start functionality. It serves a multifunctional role as a starter motor, alternator, and 15-kW engine power booster, while also helping to iron out residual crankshaft vibrations. Electric energy storage is provided by a 42-cell, 300-volt, lithium-ion battery bank. Its performance is carefully monitored and governed by an electronic control unit, through which electric current from the engine is fed. To optimize the engine's

> **Boosters**
>
> Operating auxiliary power units, such as power steering and power brakes, by electricity rather than using a power take-off from the gasoline engine crankshaft is a growing trend in conventional cars.

fuel-saving capacity, auxiliary functions, such as the water pump, air conditioning, and power steering systems, were removed from the engine's belt drive, and instead they are electrically powered.

Expressing pride in its concept's environmental benefits, Saab seems even more proud of the vehicle's sporty characteristics. With its 260-horsepower, 2.0-liter turbo BioPower engine and 53-kW electric motors, the special Saab 9-3 can briefly generate torque values three times greater than its gasoline-only equivalent. With automatic transmission, it is expected to achieve 0 to 62 mph acceleration in just 6.9 seconds, substantially quicker than the 8.8 seconds for the equivalent gasoline model.

An Environmental Protection Agency fuel economy figure for the concept vehicle is not available, but Saab says an estimated fuel savings of 5 to 7 percent is provided by the automatic engine stop/start function alone. Whenever the vehicle is stationary, the engine is immediately shut off to save fuel. As soon as the brake is released, it is automatically started again by the powerful ISG. In congested driving conditions such as city traffic or bumper-to-bumper freeway driving, economy is enhanced because the vehicle can travel without use of the internal combustion engine in Zero Mode. This mode can be selected by the driver using a button on the center console—it allows pure electric operation.

At speeds below 31, Zero Mode will shut off the engine and switch the car to electric power only. In this mode, the battery bank provides a range of between 6 and 12 miles. The engine is smoothly reengaged whenever the battery status approaches a low-charge level or the electronic throttle opening requires acceleration beyond the 31 mph operating limit.

Whenever the engine is shut down, all auxiliary functions, such as power steering, air conditioning, and lighting, remain unaffected because they are electrically powered through the battery not by a belt drive from the engine. The removal of the mechanical loads on the engine contributes to fuel economy and increases the vehicle's range on a full tank of fuel. In mixed city and highway driving, Saab estimates the vehicle's range as 500 miles.

Open to Criticism

This look at the Saab concept is intended to be a gaze at what might be coming into our automotive future. But there is no guarantee that this vision will ever be realized. Those with a strong environmental bent might well look at the Saab concept and at the mythical multi-hybrid vehicle I described earlier and say neither goes far enough because each still produces some harmful emissions—pollution in very minor amounts and carbon dioxide in larger measure. At the same time car company engineers and product development experts might well look at the vehicles and deride them for their incredible complication and plethora of systems. Because each system means cost, these vehicles might well be desirable intellectually but prohibitive from a cost standpoint.

One key thing to remember regarding current and future hybrid and alternative vehicles: most major car companies the world over have or can obtain the technology to develop and build highly fuel-efficient nearly zero-pollution vehicles. The final, and much harder trick, is manufacturing and selling those vehicles *at a profit*. Because car companies are (or at least hope to be) profit-making ventures, devising hybrid and alternative fuel vehicles that a large number of people will buy is a prerequisite. And so far it has seemed to be very difficult.

But times are changing. The combined realities of high fuel prices, chaos abroad, our reliance on foreign oil, and the desire to provide stewardship to our planet all speak to a growing interest in alternative fuel and hybrid vehicles. In fact, the auto market is poised for one of the most exciting eras in its history. New technologies are out there waiting to be tried, developed, and exploited. It is difficult to predict which technology will "win," but it is much easier to determine who the real winners are, because we are the winners. If you drink water and breathe air, you will benefit from hybrid and alternative fuel technology. The following chapters will provide you with details on each of the most promising technologies.

The Least You Need to Know

◆ Hybrid and alternative fuel vehicle sales are going through the roof, but as hybrids get the ink, Flex Fuel vehicles reap the sales.

◆ New diesel technology that adds clean diesel exhaust could prompt consumers to take a fresh look at this highly fuel-efficient engine type.

◆ Against long odds, nuclear power might become resurgent in the United States, prompting the development of a "smart electrical grid" that might spur a renaissance in electric vehicles.

◆ A future vehicle might well contain elements from conventional cars, hybrids, alternative fuel cars, and diesels, resulting in a vehicle offering excellent fuel economy and minimal emissions.

Gasoline–Electric Hybrid Vehicles

In This Chapter

- ◆ Getting past the "hybrid hype"
- ◆ Addressing the version 1.1 objection
- ◆ Striking the correct compromise
- ◆ Eyeballing the bottom line

It might be hard to remember back to the days before gasoline first spiked to $3 a gallon, but in those innocent days of our misspent youth, the first two gas-electric hybrid vehicles to hit the American market—the Honda Insight and the Toyota Prius—were greeted with a collective yawn. It wasn't that the vehicles weren't good. Indeed they were remarkably good, especially when compared to the pure electrics such as the GM EV1 that preceded them. But two issues prevented those first hybrids from becoming solid hits. First, neither Honda nor Toyota had the production capacity to sell more than a few thousand Insights or Priuses a year so they didn't put much marketing juice behind them. And, more important, gasoline was so inexpensive that the average consumer didn't have fuel economy on her or his radar screen.

But that changed big time when the second-generation Toyota Prius arrived as Hurricane Katrina and then an unsettled situation in the Middle East kicked gasoline prices through the roof. The Prius and Insight promised amazingly frugal fuel consumption and strong environmental benefits, so hybrids in general and the Prius in particular became media darlings. Movie stars shunned their limousines to ride to the Academy Awards in their hybrids, and TV stars such as *Curb Your Enthusiasm*'s Larry David decided to flaunt their allegiance to hybrids as a sign of their progressive thinking.

Definitions

A scientific theory speculates that **greenhouse gases,** such as carbon dioxide, trap heat in the atmosphere in much the same way that glass does in a greenhouse roof—heat can get in but it can't get out. Some say this is a cause of global warming.

At the same time, publicity about global warming and the creation of *greenhouse gases* brought more attention to the new (but not really new) idea. Because of the small size of the typical hybrid's gasoline engine, its production of pollutants, including the number one "greenhouse gas" carbon dioxide, was very small compared to conventional gasoline vehicles of similar size.

What Are Gasoline-Electric Hybrids?

While Toyota and Honda were reaping the whirlwind of positive publicity that surrounded hybrids as fuel prices rose and then rose again, the fact that the concept is at least a century old was lost in the shuffle. Also lost was the fact that back in 1993, the U.S. Department of Energy (DOE) initiated its Hybrid Electric Vehicle (HEV) program, which began as a five-year cost-shared partnership with the "Big Three" American auto manufacturers: General Motors, Ford, and DaimlerChrysler. The three U.S. automakers committed to producing production-feasible HEV propulsion systems by 1998, first-generation prototypes by 2000, and market-ready HEVs by 2003.

The push toward hybrids came in the wake of the realization that battery-powered "pure electrics" were just not going to work for most people in most situations if and until there was a breakthrough in battery technology. As the DOE put it, "Hybrid power systems were conceived as a way to compensate for the shortfall in battery technology when electric vehicles were introduced."

Because the batteries of the early '90s (and for that matter the batteries of today) were able to store only enough energy for relatively short trips, engineers determined that an onboard generator powered by an internal combustion (IC) engine could be installed and used to charge the batteries as the vehicle proceeded on its way, giving it much longer range. Early in the development process that followed, researchers biased their systems toward battery-electric power, while eschewing the internal combustion engine as a source of propulsion for the vehicle. By having the vehicle operate on "wall-plug" electricity stored in the batteries as much as possible, supplemented only when absolutely necessary by the IC engine, efficiency and emissions performance could be optimized.

The expectation was that, with better batteries, the IC engine would eventually become unnecessary. In other words, we would transition from hybrids that used an internal combustion engine to keep batteries in a ready state of charge to pure electrics that had no IC engine at all. But after 20 years of study and intense battery research, DOE says that "it seems that hybrids are taking center stage and electric vehicles are only being used in niche market applications where fewer miles are traveled."

Though not part of the DOE HEV Program, Toyota and Honda dove into hybrid research on their own. As the U.S. program moved forward, its goals began to merge with the goals of the Partnership for a New Generation of Vehicles (PNGV), which in turn morphed into the FreedomCAR program. In other words, it began to drift away from the hybrid concept. By that time the Japanese had introduced their gasoline-electric hybrid cars to the market and assumed a clear leadership position with regard to hybrid technology. The first hybrids on the market cut emissions of global-warming pollutants by a third to a half, and more recent models cut emissions by even more.

How Do Gasoline-Electric Hybrids Work?

As the federal government defines it, a hybrid electric vehicle (HEV) is a vehicle that has two sources of motive energy. What this means in practice is the use of some type of internal combustion engine combined with an electric motor (or motors) getting its (their) power from storage batteries. Unlike so-called "pure electric" vehicles, the batteries are not charged by an outside source—for example, plugging them into an electrical socket in your garage. Instead, their batteries are charged by an in-vehicle charging system. Thus, they are self-contained except for the need to refuel their internal combustion engines.

The internal combustion engine used in a typical HEV can be sized to deal with average load, not peak load, because the auxiliary stored power, usually electric battery power used to activate the electric motor, is used to deal with higher loads such as hill climbing. This has the benefit of allowing the installation of a smaller, lighter, and less fuel-thirsty engine. In addition, hybrid vehicles have regenerative braking capability, which means that during deceleration some of the energy that in conventional cars is simply dissipated as heat off the brakes is used to recharge the storage batteries.

Boosters

The regenerative braking process uses the electric motor as a generator to spin out electricity when the vehicle is slowing to a stop or simply coasting down a hill. In a conventional car this energy is wasted.

The automatic start-shutoff feature used by most current hybrid cars easily could be installed on conventional gasoline-powered vehicles. The United States DOE estimates this step alone could increase fuel economy 8 percent.

A fuel-saving feature offered by hybrids is the automatic start-shutoff. When you stop the vehicle, the system turns off the internal combustion engine. Then when you lift your foot off the brake pedal to accelerate again, the engine is restarted. Idling the engine while you're sitting still wastes energy, so this is a very sensible and reasonably easy-to-engineer step. Some sophisticated hybrid systems don't start the IC engine until your vehicle is well underway, sometimes not until it is traveling at 30 mph or so. This maximizes the fuel economy and environmental benefits of the electric drive system, and it also alleviates the possibly irritating factor of having the gasoline engine stop and start repeatedly while you are crawling through bumper-to-bumper traffic.

The combination of automatic stop-start, regenerative braking and the use of smaller, less powerful engines enables hybrid vehicles to achieve fuel efficiency that is significantly better than with gasoline-powered vehicles, while emissions are greatly decreased. The key to making all this work seamlessly is a very sophisticated computerized transmission that can channel power from two sources, the internal combustion engine and the electric motor or motors. HEVs usually operate using only the gasoline engine power, the electric motor power, or both, depending on the situation. Enabling these transitions to occur without making them irritatingly noticeable to drivers and passengers is important for doing this well.

The major difference between HEVs and "pure" EVs is the use of an internal combustion engine using conventional gasoline as fuel. By using an IC engine to keep batteries topped up and to provide some motive force, instead of relying completely on a motor-storage battery combination, HEVs can conquer the range problem that has haunted electric vehicles since time immemorial. In addition, fuel economy is phenomenal because the engine needs only to propel the vehicle at cruising speeds on flat ground. In more challenging situations, like accelerating from a stop or passing another vehicle on the highway, the battery-powered electric motor offers a significant and almost instantaneous supplement. Plus HEVs use conventional fuels, which means virtually no change in infrastructure is required for their use. You can fill the fuel tank at any local gas station.

The Version 1.1 Problem

Most of us have dealt with the now-proverbial version 1.1 issue in one way or another. Usually the scenario unfolds similar to this: you see a product such as a software program touted as the answer to your secret prayers; you rush out to buy the program; install it; and instead of solving your most vexing problem, it *becomes* your most vexing problem by crashing your system, ruining your computer, and causing disease and pestilence to spread through the world. Because so many of us have been burned by version 1.1, there is a reluctance to buy the first version of anything. In the world of automobiles, this has been epitomized by the long-held rule of thumb that predates computers—"Never buy a model the first year it's on the market."

Many people harbor a similar fear when it comes to hybrids. A study done by *Kelley Blue Book* Marketing Research found that a significant percentage of consumers had serious concerns about the advanced technology contained in HEVs, and those concerns limited their desire to buy a hybrid vehicle.

Frankly, a lot of this fear is unfounded. Because the interest in hybrids has peaked in just the past few months, many believe that HEVs are so leading-edge that they are untried, unproven technology. But in actuality, the current hybrids from Honda and Toyota are well into their second or third generations. Although the Toyota Prius has had a couple well-publicized voluntary product recalls, it and the other hybrid vehicles on the market have been remarkably trouble-free.

> **Boosters**
>
> There is a great deal of technology sharing going on in the hybrid development effort. For example, Ford Motor Company uses several Toyota patents in its hybrids, and General Motors and DaimlerChrysler are cooperating in the development of less-expensive hybrid systems.

As more manufacturers enter the hybrid marketplace, we can expect to see some product-quality stumbles. Those who feel they are late in the game might rush the development and endurance testing cycles to get their hybrids into the market, but we don't anticipate endemic catastrophic failures of upcoming hybrids either.

The Pluses and Minuses of Hybrid Vehicles

The media has been very vocal about the pluses of hybrid electric vehicles. The fuel economy they deliver is amazing versus that of a conventional car, and because of this, they can help us limit our use of increasingly scarce and expensive petroleum. Fuel economy is often at least 25 percent better than for similar gasoline-powered vehicles. HEVs also pollute much less than conventional vehicles. Estimates indicate that hybrids can deliver emission reductions of as much as 50 percent for carbon dioxide and 90 percent for carbon monoxide. The rule of thumb is that the less time the gasoline engine runs the more potential benefits, especially when it comes to the production of the greenhouse gas carbon dioxide. Most of the environmental gains come when hybrids are operating in electric-only mode, and the electric assist also boosts fuel economy performance.

The downsides of hybrids are much less publicized but very important to understand. Compared to a conventional gasoline car, a hybrid is much more complicated. In addition to its internal combustion engine, it also has a second, integrated drive system in the form of the electric motor and battery pack. One could say it has two complete drive systems, and that would be correct with the exception that both power plants channel their energy through the same transmission. There is nothing inherently wrong with complicated technology. But in the case of hybrids, complication adds weight, expense, and more systems that can fail.

Of these downsides, the most vexing problem is expense. Hybrids would be a much more cost-effective solution to a variety of fuel- and environmental-related issues if only the price could come down. That will become more obvious when we look closer at the cost-benefit analysis of hybrids later in this chapter. The main culprit is the high cost of batteries, so if a battery breakthrough were made, the price of hybrids could more closely approach that of conventional cars. Of course, a battery breakthrough might change the game so much that we wouldn't need hybrids; we could just switch to pure electric cars. More on this in Chapter 9.

Potholes

Batteries that can store enough energy to help power a 3,000-pound vehicle are very expensive and very heavy. Researchers around the globe currently are hard at work trying to perfect battery technology that will result in cheap and light electrical storage batteries.

A fact that has haunted hybrids even as they have gained unprecedented popularity in the last few years is that they don't really get the fuel mileage suggested by the Environmental Protect Agency's (EPA) fuel economy figures. That's true, but the issue is not confined to hybrid vehicles. Most vehicles seem to fail to achieve EPA-predicted levels of fuel economy in real-world driving by consumers, and the issue has grown so big that the EPA is currently revising its procedures. The positive that stems from the negative is that, regardless of the EPA figures, hybrids are significantly more fuel-efficient than conventional vehicles.

In essence, HEVs are a good (perhaps brilliant) compromise between the conventional gasoline car, which has been honed to operate nearly flawlessly but drinks precious fossil fuel and spews carbon dioxide and small amounts of other substances into the air; and the electric car, which has the near-fatal flaw of extremely limited range but the gigantic benefit of emitting virtually nothing at all. The beauty of hybrid electric vehicles is that they help improve air quality with no appreciable loss in vehicle performance, range, or safety. Most hybrid electric vehicles perform as well or better than internal combustion engine cars of similar size.

Driving a Hybrid Electric Vehicle Day-to-Day

The thing most of us who test cars for a living notice about the latest hybrid vehicles is not how different they are from conventional gasoline cars, but rather how similar they are to the cars and SUVs most of us drive these days. Many expect hybrids to be slow, but they are not slow. Many expect that they won't be fun to drive, but they can be fun to drive. Many expect that they'll be cramped and uncomfortable, but they are just as roomy and accommodating as conventional cars. One proof is that a hybrid drivetrain option is now being offered

Boosters

Performance hybrid? Isn't that an oxymoron? Nope! For example, the hybrid version of the Lexus GS sport-luxury sedan is the fastest accelerating model in the GS line.

on some of the most popular vehicle models in the country—cars like the Honda Accord and Toyota Camry. Additional proof comes from the fact that the leading luxury car maker in the United States, Lexus, offers several hybrid models in its lineup. Those vehicles—sedans and SUVs—perform as well or better than the conventional versions of each model.

Although range is the bugaboo of the electric car, range is one of the HEVs' strong suits. When you combine the typical hybrid's vastly superior fuel economy with a standard-size gasoline fuel tank, you can put a phenomenal number of miles on it before you have to stop for fuel. Driving ranges in excess of 500 miles are not uncommon versus 300 to 400 miles for a typical passenger car. Well-designed HEVs can not only accelerate as rapidly and travel as fast as conventional vehicles, they can also offer the same safety and convenience capabilities.

Safety

On the safety front, one urban myth has sprung up around hybrids that doesn't want to go away. The myth is that police and fire department emergency workers are put into mortal danger by hybrids because they carry high-voltage electrical wiring that can electrocute would-be rescuers trying to aid victims of car crashes. Though hybrids do indeed carry high-voltage batteries and wires, the reality is that the threat is not very great.

In the first place, a hybrid vehicle's high-voltage battery pack cells are sealed and protected by their metal battery cover. In addition, all high-voltage circuits and plugs for the system are marked, color-coded orange, and posted with warnings to advise of their presence, so well-trained fire-rescue teams should have few difficulties understanding the threat and avoiding it. Rescue workers routinely remove the ignition key and disconnect the vehicle's 12-volt battery immediately upon reaching an emergency situation with a conventional vehicle. Even if warnings on the car are ignored, taking these initial two steps will disable the high-voltage controller on a hybrid, essentially negating the electrocution threat.

As with all new cars and trucks sold in the United States, HEVs meet all federal motor vehicle safety requirements. Just as with conventional vehicles, they are equipped with the same seatbelts, airbags, and electronic aids like anti-lock brakes and electronic stability control systems. Stepping down in size from a full-size SUV to a smaller hybrid sedan might decrease your safety risk somewhat because vehicles with greater mass usually fare better in collisions than lighter vehicles. But there is nothing about a hybrid that is inherently unsafe. You would experience the same phenomenon if you were to switch from a big SUV to a small conventional car.

Safety and survivability are just two factors when it comes to insurance. With hybrids, the overriding factor is that they are complicated, so the cost to repair them after an accident can be high. Because of this, insurance rates for hybrids are a little higher than for conventional versions of the same make and model but the difference is often less than 5 percent.

Reliability

As we mentioned previously in this chapter, hybrid vehicles are complex pieces of machinery. Quite literally, there is a lot that can go wrong. Despite that though, hybrids have a strong reputation for reliability and longevity. As the hybrid vehicle fleet ages, it will be very interesting to see if this trend continues.

Because of the complexity of their vehicles, owners of hybrids need to keep an eye on maintenance, and frankly there is a lot to keep an eye on. First, hybrids use gasoline-fueled internal combustion engines, so you need to maintain those engines just as you would the engine in a conventional car. Hybrids require oil changes, oil-, air-, and fuel-filter changes, coolant flushes and fills, sparkplug and sparkplug wire changes, and so on. In comparison, the electric portion of the drive system will be remarkably easy to maintain, but it is still an added burden versus a conventional car.

A potentially big but largely unknown factor is the battery pack. To date, the rechargeable batteries have demonstrated a remarkable amount of staying power, and some service experts who work for the major hybrid manufacturers have told us they will last "essentially for the life of the vehicle." But if the battery does fail, know this—it will be very expensive to replace.

Cost to Repair

Hybrids are relatively rare; they use specialized parts, and they require special skills to repair them. This is the formula for high cost of repair. But in the current crop of hybrids we haven't really seen that. Why? Because the manufacturers of hybrids offer lengthy drivetrain (engine and transmission) warranties and special service programs to make certain their early hybrid customers don't get burned and spread negative word-of-mouth.

Still, as the hybrid fleet ages, we can only guess what will happen as warranties expire and customers drift away from the dealers for their service needs. We expect that, just as there are specialized shops for diesels and for vehicles of a specific brand, there will also be hybrid-specialty repair shops. Again, you can expect the prices these specialists charge will not be cheap.

Cost to Operate

So far the cost to operate hybrid vehicles has been extremely low. It is not as low as for pure electric vehicles, because you still have to fill hybrids with expensive gasoline at least occasionally. But compared to gasoline vehicles, the cost-per-mile (not factoring in the purchase price) is much lower. This is almost entirely the result of the fact that hybrids can deliver up to 50 percent better fuel economy than their nonhybrid sister models or equivalents. Other costs to operate are very similar to those of operating a conventional gasoline vehicle.

Purchase Price

What price are you willing to pay to save money? This seemingly self-contradictory query is the logical one prospective buyers of hybrid vehicles should be asking themselves. Partially the product of hype and partially the product of the fear that gasoline prices will go still higher, hybrid vehicles definitely are commanding premium prices versus their gas-fired equivalents. There also are waiting lists to buy some hybrid models.

The reasons for the higher prices have been alluded to in this chapter. First, hybrids are more complicated to engineer and build than conventional cars, and they use special parts, most notably expensive batteries. Second, hybrids cost less to operate, because they use far less gasoline than conventional vehicles. And finally, hybrids are hot, cool, and environmentally friendly, and a lot of people like those attributes. These days a percentage of the buying public absolutely has to have a hybrid, and because supply of many of the models is still short of demand, dealers can get premium prices.

How much is that premium? For the hottest hybrid cars and trucks it is in the neighborhood of 20 to 30 percent of the Manufacturers Suggested Retail Price (MSRP). But as supply catches up with demand, the premiums should lessen or disappear altogether. But for now, the premiums often make it unlikely that you will come out ahead of the gasoline-vehicle buyer at the conclusion of the typical five-year ownership period.

Do Hybrids Make Sense Economically?

In the wake of the media coverage of hybrids, a major controversy developed. At its crux is the contention, as some have said, "hybrids don't make economic sense." When you step back from that assertion for a minute and look at it without bias, the case could be made that darn few of the consumer products we buy and aspire to buy make economic sense. Does it make economic sense to buy bottled water instead of drinking from the tap? To buy designer jeans rather than no-name dungarees? To stay in a five-star hotel rather than the motel across the tracks? The same holds true in the selection of your personal vehicle. Does it make economic sense to buy a luxury car? To get leather seats? To option up to a 14-speaker stereo?

Interestingly this whole debate has become emotionally and politically charged. Proponents of hybrids support the concept of hybrids for many good reasons including concern for the environment and our nation's future, and they strike hard at those who contend hybrids don't "pencil." Although those that defend hybrids on all fronts from all criticism are well-intentioned, there is certainly no harm in examining the dollars-and-sense of owning a hybrid vehicle versus a conventional vehicle dispassionately. If you look at the matter without prejudice, you might well find that the purchase of a hybrid won't save you money but that the purchase will be a good and worthy choice anyway.

All that is prelude to the following discussion. It is confined to discovering if, within strictly economic parameters, a hybrid will save you money in your individual circumstances. As can be seen from information provided earlier in this chapter, the projected "savings" over the ownership cycle of a hybrid versus a gasoline-powered vehicle hinges in large measure on how much of a premium you pay for the hybrid. As we have seen, the premium often amounts to several thousand dollars. That, frankly, is a lot of money to make up in fuel cost savings even in these days of high gasoline prices.

Figuring Your Ownership Cycle

To make a determination on the advisability of purchasing a hybrid vehicle rather than a gasoline vehicle given your situation, it is beneficial to put in some vehicle ownership-cost parameters to allow you to do a meaningful comparison.

First, determine how much you are paying for the vehicle and how much you expect it to be worth when you are ready to sell it. Second, determine how many miles a year you will drive. Third, estimate how much gasoline will cost on average during your ownership period.

Potholes

How can you determine what fuel costs will be in the future? You can't, but you have to take educated guesses and run a couple "what if" situations to get a handle on the potential cost benefits of HEVs.

Are There Real Savings?

After you have these parameters in mind, test a hypothesis or two to see if the purchase of a hybrid will make economic sense for you. Remember, you can tailor these examples to your own situation and expectations of the future, but even if you don't, they will provide a good comparative look at the relative merits of each purchase.

To make these hypothetical scenarios relatively simple, let's assume that the resale value of the hybrid will be 5 percent more than the equivalent gasoline car will be at the end of the 5-year ownership period. Let's further assume that you will drive either car 12,000 miles a year or 60,000 miles after 5 years, and that gasoline will average $3-a-gallon for the same period. In our illustration let's specify that the EPA mileage rating for the hybrid is 50 miles per gallon while the equivalent gasoline car gets 35 mpg, which is representative of the real-world figures.

With all this in place, let's calculate the projected cost for both vehicles. Based on our outlined scenario, you will burn 1,714 gallons of gasoline to travel your 60,000 miles in the conventional car, and at 3 bucks-a-gallon that will cost you $5,142. Or, if you buy the hybrid version of the vehicle, you will burn 1,200 gallons of $3-a-gallon gas, costing you $3,600 to rack up the same number of miles.

Obviously, in terms of total fuel cost the hybrid has the advantage, and by quite a large margin. But the analysis isn't complete yet. Let us further assume that the purchase price of the hybrid was $30,000 while the purchase price of the gasoline-powered version of the vehicle was $25,000. At resale time 5 years down the road, let's assume the gasoline version is worth $10,000 and the hybrid is worth 5 percent more or $10,500. What this means is the premium you paid for the hybrid was $4,500. To determine your profit or loss by buying a hybrid, you compare the fuel cost savings—$1,542—to the price premium—$4,500. In this case the hybrid represents a $2,958 loss. Tax credits and governmental incentives, which vary widely but strongly favor hybrids, can be the difference-maker here. Combined tax and cash benefits of $3,000, not beyond the realm of possibility in the ever-changing world of government-sponsored incentives, would turn the net loss into a winner.

Things also can change considerably if you make different assumptions. For the sake of argument, let's assume $4-a-gallon gasoline. With this simple change in assumptions, the gasoline version of the car will burn $6,856 in fuel in a typical 5-year ownership period, and the hybrid will use just $4,800 in fuel. In light of the $4,500 purchase price premium, that represents $2,444 net cost disadvantage for the hybrid. Again, tax rebates and government cash incentives can make up this relatively small amount, which is less than $40 a month during the 5-year ownership term.

Who Benefits?

Who benefits from hybrids? Every time someone buys a hybrid we all benefit, because that purchase can help improve the quality of our air and lessen our reliance on fossil fuels. On a more personal basis—this is, after all, the generation of me, me, me—if you want to determine if you would benefit from owning a hybrid we recommend strongly that you take a long, hard look at how much you drive, what kind of driving you do, and how much you value contributing to a cleaner environment and helping defuse our thirst for oil.

Looking strictly at the economics, a long-distance commuter who spends a lot of time in bumper-to-bumper freeway and/or stop-and-go city traffic is the best candidate for maximizing the benefits of a hybrid. An HEV has the unique characteristic of getting better fuel economy in city driving than on highways because in city driving it can often operate primarily as an electric and the engine stop-start feature can be brought to bear. This coincides quite nicely with the pleasant fact that hybrid vehicles can legally drive in carpool lanes in many areas with just the driver aboard, a serious timesaver in dense urban traffic.

On the other hand, if you drive most of your miles at highway speeds, a hybrid's cost-benefits to you will diminish, though it will still do better than a conventional gas car in terms of overall fuel cost. If you don't drive much, you won't benefit much either.

Guide to Currently Available Models

A guide to the currently available HEVs is relatively short but new hybrid models are being added to the market frequently.

Toyota Prius

It wasn't the first hybrid in America, but in its second generation it came to epitomize the entire class.

Honda Civic Hybrid

Building a hybrid version of the top-selling Honda Civic was a leap of faith for Honda, but now the vehicle has become a mainstay.

Ford Escape Hybrid

The first modern hybrid from an American manufacturer, the Escape hybrid was also the first hybrid SUV.

Mercury Mariner Hybrid

A kissing cousin to the Ford Escape Hybrid, the Mercury Mariner Hybrid has a slightly higher level of equipment, luxury, and style.

Honda Accord Hybrid

Ultimate fuel economy is not the strong suit of the Accord Hybrid. Instead it delivers V6-like performance with fuel economy that is just slightly better than the conventional four-cylinder version of the car.

Lexus RX 400h

The first luxury hybrid, the RX 400h also is the best-performing RX model. As with the Accord, its fuel economy performance is good, but not stellar.

Lexus GS 450h

The GS 450h is the first performance-oriented hybrid, so its fuel economy and emissions performance are secondary to its added power and longer range.

Saturn Vue Green Line

In an effort to bring hybrid technology to a larger group of buyers, the Vue Green Line uses simpler hybrid technology, which lowers its price but limits its benefits.

The Least You Need to Know

◆ A hybrid electric vehicle uses a small gasoline engine to charge its onboard batteries and propel the vehicle. An electric motor powered by the batteries supplements the gasoline engine, increasing fuel efficiency markedly.

◆ Hybrid vehicles offer significant benefits in both vastly increased fuel efficiency and significantly lower exhaust emissions.

◆ Hybrid vehicles represent an excellent compromise between a conventional gasoline-powered car and a pure electric car.

◆ When considering the purchase of a hybrid, weigh the positive benefits of reducing the consumption of fossil fuels and the emission of greenhouse gases as part of your analysis.

Chapter 5

Flex Fuel/E85 Vehicles

In This Chapter

- ◆ Learning other ways to skin the cat
- ◆ Finding fuel you can grow
- ◆ Determining a cost-effective solution
- ◆ Discovering the dollars and sense of E85

When it comes to vehicles that can lessen our reliance on off-shore petroleum and improve the quality of the air we breathe, hybrids, popular as they are right now, are not the only game in town. In fact, one potential answer to the fuel economy/clean air/fossil fuel conundrum predates the initial modern hybrid. The shorthand for the technology is Flex Fuel—vehicles that can burn conventional gasoline but also can be powered by a mix of gasoline and ethanol that is called E85.

Though there were many Flex Fuel vehicles (FFVs) on the market well before the introduction of the first modern gasoline-electric hybrids, it turns out the debut of hybrids was the best thing that could have ever happened to vehicles capable of running on a strong mix of ethanol. Why? Well, the advent of gasoline-electric hybrid cars might not have changed our reliance on foreign sources of oil, much improved the quality of the air we breathe, or done a great deal to reduce the amount of fossil fuel we use for transportation. However, one thing they did do, almost immediately, was capture the attention and admiration of the American public.

Because the hybrids seem to be a logical step in the right direction, toward lower exhaust emissions and away from our perpetual thirst for petroleum, they have been greeted by the American public with enthusiasm. No, not every American wants to buy one, at least not yet, but consumer studies show that a high percentage of Americans are more than willing to consider one, and that percentage will almost certainly rise as a wider variety of hybrid models come to market. This, in turn, influenced the American manufacturers who were the key producers of Flex Fuel vehicles to (you should pardon the expression) flex their environmental muscles by promoting ethanol, the Flex Fuel concept, and its environmental benefits.

Why Flex Fuel Vehicles?

Based on their location in the Midwest, it is not hard to see why America's automakers have gravitated to Flex Fuel vehicles that use ethanol as their answer to the gasoline-electric hybrids that have been championed by the Japanese. After all, the vast majority of the ethanol produced in this country is derived from corn, and legislators in Corn Belt states are pushing ethanol's use to boost the fortunes of their constituents with favorable laws, regulations, and subsidies. Although FFVs have been boosted as logical substitutes for hybrids, the two dueling technologies differ in both cost and benefits.

> **Boosters**
>
> The most important of the regulations favoring ethanol-capable vehicles is the Environmental Protection Agency's (EPA) rule that rewards auto manufacturers for building them, even if they operate on gasoline. Some say this has actually increased gasoline use in the last several years.

When operated on the ethanol-heavy E85, Flex Fuel vehicles deliver positives that include lower exhaust emissions and a lessening of our country's reliance on oil—two benefits also claimed by hybrids. But unlike hybrids, which are fueled with conventional gasoline, Flex Fuel vehicles require the use of a special and often hard-to-obtain fuel to offer the above-mentioned benefits. Running on gasoline, as so many do in every-day life, they offer none of these positives and are, for all intents and purposes, comparable to other cars, trucks, and SUVs.

What Is Ethanol?

At the most basic level, ethanol is grain alcohol not far removed from what you find in a bottle of Jack Daniels or Old Grand-Dad. Though it can be produced from a number of sources, in the United States the most popular source material in its production is corn. The corn is crushed and mixed into a "mash" that is distilled to produce ethanol, which, among other things, is highly flammable and thus a good fuel.

Though some prefer the benefits of sippin' whiskey, ethanol's key benefits when used as a fuel are that it is clean-burning, has a high octane rating, and is produced from renewable sources. Because it is domestically manufactured from American-grown crops, ethanol can help reduce America's dependence on foreign sources of energy.

What Is E85?

Although some vehicles, including Henry Ford's legendary Model T, could operate quite happily on 100 percent pure ethanol, it is not generally used as a motor fuel. Instead, a percentage of ethanol is combined with unleaded gasoline, enabling the fuel to offer many of the benefits of gasoline while adding many of the benefits of ethanol.

This use of ethanol/gasoline blends can be beneficial because the addition of ethanol can decrease the fuel's cost and will almost certainly decrease the harmful exhaust emissions produced by burning gasoline. It also increases the fuel's octane rating, which means the fuel is less likely to detonate (in common parlance *ping*) in the combustion chamber.

> **? Definitions**
>
> When an internal combustion engine **pings**, it means the air-fuel mixture in the combustion chamber is exploding rather than burning. Also called knock, ping can damage your engine, sometimes making holes in the piston.

This, in turn, means the engine can be tuned for better fuel economy and/or enhanced power.

Even though you might not be aware of it, the gasoline in your car's gas tank right now likely includes ethanol. Because lead and the compound MTBE were banned as fuel additives designed to prevent "knock" or "ping," ethanol has been routinely used for that purpose. In the vast majority of cases, this fuel is a 90 percent gasoline–10 percent ethanol mix called, not very imaginatively, E10. E10 is approved for use in any make or model of vehicle sold in the United States, and many automakers recommend its use because of its high performance, clean-burning characteristics. These days, almost half of America's gasoline is blended with ethanol, most in this 10 percent variety, and its use is climbing.

Although FFVs can use E10 as fuel, E10 does not offer any more in the way of benefits compared to other unleaded gasolines. Instead, FFVs offer their real benefits when they burn E85, the 85 percent ethanol–15 percent unleaded gasoline mix.

What Are Flex Fuel Vehicles?

One of the greatest advantages of Flex Fuel vehicles is they function almost exactly the way a conventional gasoline-powered car does. That shouldn't be surprising, because the technology is virtually the same. FFVs use the same internal combustion engines that power today's conventional cars, and their fuel systems are only slightly modified. Because E85 is more corrosive than pure gasoline and has a solvent effect on some plastics and rubber products, things such as hoses and fittings that might be affected are replaced by pieces of different materials. FFVs also require a special sensor in the fuel system to analyze the fuel mixture and control the fuel injection and timing to adjust for different fuel compositions. Neither modification is very expensive; meaning the cost of converting the current fleet of vehicles to use E85 is minimal. This can translate to a good cost/benefit ratio for you and me as consumers.

The key advantages FFVs offer are lower exhaust emissions and potentially lower fuel costs (dependent, of course, on the price of E85 versus gasoline). Because E85 has the highest oxygen content of the commonly available fuels, it burns more completely leaving fewer byproducts. The

EPA says making the switch from gasoline to ethanol blends can lower poisonous carbon monoxide levels by as much as 40 percent and smog-forming pollutants such as nitrous oxides by 15 percent. The use of E85 is also effective in reducing so-called greenhouse gases by as much as 30 percent versus burning gasoline. This could serve to help reduce the greenhouse effect some claim is a key culprit in global warming.

As we said, Flex Fuel technology predates the reintroduction of gasoline-electric hybrids by several years. Ford Motor Company is acknowledged by the EPA as the originator of the technology, but it was quickly adopted by the other American manufacturers. Very quietly, each of the "Big Three" (Ford, General Motors, and Chrysler) has built about 1.5 million of the vehicles since their introduction in the late 1980s, and there are an estimated 5 million FFVs on American roads today. That is a substantial number that dwarfs the total of hybrids on American roads. The rub is that in every-day use many of these FFVs are using conventional gasoline as fuel, which eliminates their advantages.

Globally, estimates are that there are some 10 million FFVs in use. One country that has put special emphasis on Flex Fuel and ethanol vehicles is Brazil, which made the political decision to foster alternative fuels so it could help control its own energy destiny decades ago. In that country more than 90 percent of the vehicles use ethanol, which is derived mostly from locally grown sugar cane.

How Do Flex Fuel Vehicles Work?

With the exception of the fuels they can use, Flex Fuel vehicles operate in exactly the same manner as conventional gasoline-powered vehicles. Similar engine and transmission technology is employed, which makes adding Flex Fuel capability to additional models very easy. The key difference is the modification to the fuel delivery system that includes the addition of a fuel-type sensor and changes to fittings and hoses to allow them to live with ethanol.

Potholes

Though the EPA acknowledges that Flex Fuel vehicles can lessen air pollution, the agency doesn't seem to feel the potential contribution is very large. As evidence, it rates the Chevrolet Impala Flex Fuel vehicle just a 6 on its 10-point air pollution scale.

The E85 fuel is delivered to the engine's combustion chambers via a fuel-injector just as it is in today's gasoline engines. The fuel sensor allows the ignition system to calibrate itself for the slight differences in the combustion characteristics between gasoline and E85. Both fuels can be stored in the same fuel tank, and there is no harm done by mixing gasoline with E85. In such a mix, however, you do lose some of the benefits of using E85 fuels.

The Pluses and Minuses of Flex Fuel Vehicles

One way to look at Flex Fuel vehicles is that they take current automotive technology and make it a measure or two better in several important areas. The ethanol that fuels them is domestically produced so it could play an important factor in limiting our country's purchases of foreign oil. When running on E85, FFVs emit significantly less pollutants than conventional gasoline vehicles, so the potential environmental benefits are real. And depending on the relative prices of gasoline and ethanol, E85 may be less expensive over time than gasoline. When you add to that the fact that adding Flex Fuel capability to new conventional vehicles is relatively inexpensive, you can see why there is enthusiasm for Flex Fuel in many circles today.

So what are the negatives? From the cost side, there are significant concerns about whether E85 will be less expensive to produce than gasoline if and when it becomes a mainstream fuel. Here's the background—gasoline is derived from petroleum in a relatively inexpensive process. Oil comes from the ground; it is pumped to "cracking plants" where gasoline and other products are produced using a fairly simple and well-understood process. Though experts differ on the details, the process to make ethanol is regarded as more complicated and, perhaps, more expensive. Some say the production of ethanol results in a net energy loss when taking in consideration the energy required to produce it, while others say the process is actually more efficient than that for making gasoline. The proof will be told when ethanol production ramps up to much higher levels, the kind of levels that would enable it to become a widely used motor vehicle fuel. For now, it's safe to say that ethanol offers no significant cost advantages and might even cost you more.

Another drawback is that on a gallon-to-gallon basis, E85 packs less punch than gasoline. When used in vehicle engines, the energy shortfall is between 12 and 25 percent, which means it takes significantly more E85 than conventional gasoline to travel the same distance.

A final negative revolves around availability. Although there are gasoline stations virtually everywhere, only a relative few of them have installed E85 pumps. Out of 167,476 retail gasoline stations nationwide, just 897 sell E85 at this writing, according to the National Ethanol Vehicle Coalition. Even though the number of fueling stations that offer E85 is growing and enthusiasm is building for Flex Fuel vehicles, the high cost of installing E85 pumps could limit individual gasoline station owners' interest in servicing the expanding interest in the fuel.

In the case of Flex Fuel vehicles, the lack of infrastructure to support them is not quite as crippling as it would be to new-technology vehicles that use a single fuel other than the standard offerings of gasoline and diesel, because the vehicles will operate just fine on gasoline. The problem is that if millions of FFVs are using gasoline, then their owners and the community at large do not benefit from their potential advantages.

Potholes

The trade publication *Automotive News* has reported that the cost for a gas station owner to install an E85 fuel pump is around $100,000.

Driving a Flex Fuel Vehicle Day-to-Day

Driving a Flex Fuel vehicle is no different than driving a conventional gasoline-powered vehicle. In fact, experts estimate that hundreds of thousands of American drivers are piloting FFVs right now without even knowing they have Flex Fuel capabilities. Although FFVs sold today often feature exterior badges and yellow fuel caps that identify them as vehicles capable of using E85, many that were sold in the 1990s are visually identical to their gasoline-only cousins. Drivers of these cars and trucks are routinely filling their tanks with gasoline, not even knowing they have an alternative that is more environmentally friendly. Although that is lamentable, the bottom line is that an FFV will feel similar to the gasoline-only version of the same model.

Safety

You might intuit from the above that FFVs' safety performance is comparable to similar models from the same manufacturer, and you'd be right. The FFV capability has no positive or negative effect on safety.

Good news on the insurance front is that FFV technology is so similar to that of conventional cars that rates for conventional cars apply. Yes, FFVs do include a few specialty parts but only the fuel sensor could be considered expensive, and it is not prone to damage in a collision.

Reliability

The fact that millions of FFVs are on American roads today is a testament to their reliability and longevity, despite many owners not being aware of their FFV status. It would not be overly optimistic to expect 100,000 miles of trouble-free service from a Flex Fuel vehicle that was properly maintained.

No special maintenance regimen is required either. An FFV can be serviced and maintained just as a conventional vehicle. FFVs are so flexible that they don't have to operate on E85 and will suffer no decline in performance or longevity if they are operated on gasoline or a gasoline-E85 mix in virtually any combination.

Cost to Repair

Under the hood, Flex Fuel vehicles are so close to their conventional gasoline-powered siblings that the cost-to-repair experience will be very similar as well. The only bit of real technology that separates a Flex Fuel vehicle from a conventional vehicle is its fuel-sensing system. Happily, these are not prone to problems, and if they fail they are not break-the-bank expensive to replace.

Some mechanics might shy away from FFVs because they are a tiny bit different from conventional cars, but in most instances, repair facilities are happy to work on them and will not charge you more for the service.

Cost to Operate

It would be nice to offer a blanket statement on an FFV's cost to operate but, unfortunately, that is impossible. The major reason is that the availability of E85 to the consumer is currently so spotty that those gas stations that have it can charge pretty much what they want. And lest you think that all E85 station owners are prone to "gouging" the public, you might be interested to learn that many of them are selling the product at a lower margin than gasoline and diesel in an attempt to serve their customers and "prime the pump" to encourage the use of the fuel.

The fierce competition between gasoline stations keeps the price of gasoline within well-defined parameters in each market in which it is sold. There are price differences between regions, but these are caused by factors such as state and local taxes and the peculiarities of the infrastructure within each region. Although E85 is affected by the same type of local and regional factors, its availability is so localized now that prices vary widely. Some stations price it above the price of gasoline, because they can, while others price it well below gasoline in an effort to boost sales.

Boosters

According to reliable sources, there are about 175,000 gasoline filling stations in the United States. DOE and the American auto manufacturers are now working to persuade more of them to offer E85.

One important factor to keep in mind is Flex Fuel vehicles suffer a fuel-economy penalty of 25 to 30 percent when they use E85 fuel. This is a significant negative factor when you compare FFVs to hybrids. Hybrids offer EPA fuel economy numbers that are startling better than comparable conventional vehicles, and Flex Fuel vehicles deliver fuel economy numbers that are lower than gasoline vehicles by a significant percentage. The National Ethanol Vehicle Coalition pegs that shortfall at 10 to 15 percent, but others suggest it is far higher, as much as 30 percent.

With this in mind, E85 has to be priced much lower than gasoline to make using it a break-even proposition, and priced a lot less to provide you cost savings. Although it is hard to generalize given the fact that E85 pricing is not as rational and easy-to-categorize as gasoline, Flex Fuel vehicles will likely cost you more per mile than if you ran the same vehicle on gasoline. Further, that doesn't include the small premium you might have to pay to obtain a vehicle with Flex Fuel capabilities.

Purchase Price

Those who are used to seeing premium prices for hybrid versions of various vehicle models will be pleased to learn that Flex Fuel capability rarely commands much of a premium in the marketplace. The additional steps to add the ability are very simple, and there are advantages to the manufacturers to offer such vehicles in the form of Corporate Average Fuel Economy requirements. This means that you can get an FFV for about the same initial outlay as a conventional gasoline-powered vehicle. Often Flex Fuel capabilities are only available on higher-level engine choices that cost more than base engines, but that is not always the case.

Projected Real Savings During the Ownership Cycle

Determining if an FFV will make economic sense for you is both simple and complicated. It is simple because there is not much downside risk in buying an FFV version of one of the many models out there that offers the technology. There is little, if any, price premium to pay for the technology and, if it turns out that E85 is unavailable or prohibitively expensive in your area, you can always operate the vehicle on gasoline. No gain but no loss either. And if E85 is significantly less expensive you could realize real gains. The complicated part involves predicting the prices of gasoline, ethanol, E85, and, for that matter, corn during the course of your ownership cycle. As commodities, those prices are subject to change at will.

Beyond the strict dollars-and-sense issues, you have to determine for yourself the value you place on helping your country and your planet with lower exhaust emissions, contributions to the environment, and a lessened reliance on foreign sources of fuel.

Figuring Your Ownership Cycle

To see if a Flex Fuel vehicle makes basic economic sense, you must put in place the vehicle ownership cost parameters we outlined in Chapter 4. To repeat, first determine how much you are paying for the vehicle and how much you expect it to be worth when you are ready to sell it. Second, determine how many miles a year you will drive. Third, estimate how much E85 and gasoline will cost during your ownership period.

Are There Real Savings?

It would be nice to give you a yes or no answer, but the reality is that we don't know enough to do that. Nobody does, because the prices of the key commodities involved—crude oil, gasoline, corn, and ethanol— are volatile and subject to outside forces such as drought and political unrest.

That does not mean, however, that it is impossible to test a few hypotheses to take a run at the answer that will fit your circumstances. To make these hypotheses relatively simple, let's assume that the resale value of the FFV and the equivalent gasoline car will be the same at the end of the 5-year ownership period. Let's further assume that you will drive either car 12,000 miles a year or 60,000 miles after 5 years. Finally, let's assume $3-a-gallon gasoline for the 5-year period and a $2.50-a-gallon E85. The EPA mileage for the FFV is 23 miles per gallon and the equivalent gasoline car gets 30 mpg combined. That makes the cost analysis relatively easy to figure. Based on our assumptions, you will burn 2,000 gallons of gasoline to travel your 60,000 miles, and at 3 bucks-a-gallon that will cost you $6,000. Or if you buy the Flex Fuel vehicle, you will burn 2,609 gallons of $2.50-a-gallon E85, costing you $6,523 to rack up the same number of miles.

Because we can further assume the purchase costs of the two vehicles were equal, the gasoline vehicle is more economical than operating an FFV on E85. On the other hand, if you operate the FFV on gasoline you'd be exactly where you'd be in a gasoline car, plus you'd have the added advantage of using E85 if you want to.

That alone is a benefit for the Flex Fuel vehicle, and things change substantially if you assume $4-a-gallon gasoline and $3-a-gallon E85. With these assumptions the gasoline car will burn $8,000 in fuel in the typical 5-year ownership period, and the FFV will use just $7,827 in fuel. The savings are hardly life-changing, but they are real. Obviously, the key to cost-effectiveness is the relative prices of gasoline and E85.

Who Benefits?

Because FFVs generally cost no more than conventional vehicles that lack the ability to use E85, you can opt into the green car realm with no additional upfront costs. If E85 is significantly less expensive than gasoline in your area, you can try using it to determine whether you have substantial fuel cost savings.

But potential cost savings are just one of the benefits of Flex Fuel vehicles. By using domestically made ethanol, it lessens our reliance on foreign oil sources; another plus. It's hard to put a dollar figure on that, of course, but many individuals seem to want to "do their part" by using E85, even if it hits them in the pocketbook.

The same holds true for the environmental benefits. Helping to mitigate global warming and at the same time limiting the emissions of harmful substances has real value, although it is hard to put a dollar sign against it.

Who won't benefit from a Flex Fuel vehicle? Well, if gasoline is cheaper in your area than E85, you won't gain any economic benefit from buying an FFV. On the other hand, it won't cost you any more either. And if you buy an FFV and fuel it with gasoline, none of us will gain any benefit, though it won't do any more harm than a gasoline car either.

Currently Available Models

Flex Fuel capability currently is offered on more than two dozen models, virtually all of them from the domestic "Big Three" automakers—General Motors, Ford Motor Company, and DaimlerChrysler. Most of the vehicles are medium to large cars, trucks, and sport utility vehicles that get average to poor fuel economy. Each model has the same attributes and performs in the same way as its gasoline-only cousins with the exception that when operated on E85 fuel, each will turn in poorer fuel economy figures. There are more details in Appendix D.

The Least You Need to Know

♦ FFVs can operate on both gasoline and a gasoline-ethanol mix called E85.

♦ FFVs offer lower exhaust emissions when operated on E85, but they offer no anti-pollution benefits when operated on gasoline.

♦ You won't pay more for an FFV than for an equivalent gasoline vehicle, so you can buy into the technology without any risk.

♦ Potential cost savings revolve around the relative prices of gasoline and E85, and those prices are difficult to predict.

Chapter 6

Natural Gas Vehicles

In This Chapter

- ◆ Discovering a hidden treasure
- ◆ Being similar to gasoline, only cleaner
- ◆ Knowing where to get gas
- ◆ Utilizing the cost benefits of a utility

Gasoline-electric hybrids have become media darlings as gasoline prices have shot up. With celebrities jumping on the hybrid bandwagon, they have become the go-to vehicle when Americans think of fuel savings with a positive environmental spin. Meanwhile, with American farmers and farm state legislators on their team, Flex Fuel/ethanol-powered vehicles are also gaining steam, especially in America's heartland. But natural gas, a fuel which some experts say is a neglected treasure, could well have equal or even greater promise than both of the more highly publicized technologies in solving the issues of high fuel cost and environmental concerns.

Though many people use natural gas to heat their homes and cook their meals, most don't consider it as a fuel for their cars.

This is true despite the fact that if they travel in big-city downtowns these days they are very likely to see natural gas-powered transit buses and garbage trucks. The fact is natural gas offers a number of advantages as a motor vehicle fuel. First, it burns very clean, providing positives on the environmental front. Second, it works well in conventional internal combustion engines, requiring only minor modifications. And third, there is a lot of it, both here in the United States and in friendly countries in South America, the Caribbean, and farther overseas.

What Is Natural Gas?

The bulk of the natural gas we use in this country comes from the ground, much like petroleum. Prospecting and drilling for it is in many ways similar to finding "Texas Tea." It's often found in oil fields, interspersed with petroleum, and in coal beds, interspersed with coal. Though it is a gas, not a liquid, natural gas can be recovered in much the same way as oil, by inserting pipes into the underground "pockets" where it is confined.

The natural gas we burn in our stoves and buses is primarily methane whose chemical symbol is CH_4 (an atom of carbon with four atoms of hydrogen). Because methane also is produced by rotting vegetation, as well as farting cows, it can be considered renewable. If you want to see methane being generated by natural forces, go to a local waste dump that has been partially covered with earth. Odds are there will be stacks to vent the recently brewed methane, which is then burned off. You won't notice much smoke because it burns so clean. Solid waste, manure, and even waste-water filled with sludge can be good producers of methane, and instead of going up in flames, the gas can be captured and used to propel our cars. According to the U.S. Energy Information Administration, 84 percent of the natural gas we use in our country comes from our country. In contrast, less than 40 percent of the crude oil we gulp each year is produced here in the United States. If one of our nation's goals is energy independence, natural gas is a huge positive.

The U.S. does import some natural gas, but most of it comes from our neighbor to the north, Canada, and our neighbor to the south, Mexico. This makes sense because natural gas is more complicated than crude oil to ship. The process involves cooling the gas until it isn't a gas anymore. Then the liquefied natural gas (LNG) is pumped into tankers and shipped to our shores. This process and the fact that LNG is imported make it more expensive than domestically produced natural gas. Though we have yet to use natural gas to power our cars, it not only heats our homes but is also used to generate a large portion of our electricity in the United States. That and industrial uses keep natural gas in high demand, which has prompted the search for overseas sources of the fuel.

Biogas, which can be produced from waste products, is vastly underutilized, yet it holds a great deal of promise in reducing our reliance on less renewable sources of energy. General Motors is America's largest user of biogas. By using landfill gas, the giant corporation recently reduced its consumption of conventional natural gas and other energy sources by 25 percent at seven of its plants.

> **Definitions**
>
> **Biogas**, a slang scientific term similar to biodiesel, covers the variations of methane that go under the aliases swamp gas, marsh gas, and digester gas. One has to wonder if the last is more than a silly pun.

What Are Natural Gas Vehicles?

Natural gas vehicles use internal combustion engines that have been modified to use methane rather than gasoline as fuel. The key advantage they offer is very clean exhaust emissions. When burned in engines, natural gas produces significantly less carbon monoxide (you know, the stuff that kills you) and nitrous oxides (the stuff that helps produce smog when exposed to sunlight). The Department of Energy (DOE) pegs those figures as 90 percent less carbon monoxide and 60 percent less nitrous oxides. Additionally, natural gas does a good job of not creating a gas we used to be unconcerned about—carbon dioxide (CO_2). Because carbon dioxide has been linked by some to the phenomenon of global warming, we now pay attention to it much more, and natural gas vehicles produce approximately 35 percent less CO_2 than conventional gasoline vehicles.

Boosters

Natural gas cars emit much less "greenhouse gas" than a typical car. For example, a Honda Civic GX is predicted to produce just 4.7 tons of greenhouse gas in a year's worth of driving versus 14.9 tons for the worst passenger vehicles on the road.

Natural gas vehicles require none of the computer-controlled rocket science wizardry that attracts some to gasoline-electric hybrids. Their engines function almost exactly as gasoline engines. Though you probably shouldn't try it over a weekend, it wouldn't take a whole lot of effort to convert your present gasoline car to natural gas.

Several major auto manufacturers build natural gas-powered car models. Unfortunately, most of them are not for sale to the general public in the United States. There are around 150,000 natural gas vehicles (NGVs) in use in the United States, but the vast majority of them are in corporate fleets rather than in private hands. Although 150,000 might seem like a big number, it is just a tiny percentage of the estimated 130 million cars in operation here in the United States.

Globally, estimates are that there are more than 4 million natural gas vehicles in use. Again, that seems like a large number until you realize that there are some 700 million cars on the road around the world.

Some countries, however, have made stronger strides in adopting natural gas cars than we have. Brazil, which has a history of promoting alternative fuel vehicles, has several hundred thousand natural gas-powered cars on the road, and the technology is becoming more prevalent in neighboring Argentina as well. In Japan a high percentage of taxis are powered by natural gas.

When it comes to larger vehicles such as transit buses, natural gas is winning favor around the world. Places as disparate as India and Italy are shifting from diesel-powered buses to natural gas, and the same is true here in the United States of America.

How Do Natural Gas Vehicles Work?

NGVs operate similar to your standard-issue gasoline-powered car. They can utilize almost identical engine and transmission technology, which is very good news for auto manufacturers. The major difference is in the fuel storage and fuel delivery systems. Instead of a gas tank, natural gas is stored in a cylinder not unlike what you'd see hooked to a backyard grill. The natural gas is delivered to the engine's combustion chambers in measured amounts rather than in atomized squirts as in the fuel-injected gasoline engines of today. The key difference is that natural gas is already in a gaseous state, which aids in its burning cleaner, while gasoline has to be mixed with air prior to its combustion, producing somewhat more residual waste products.

> **Boosters**
>
> When it comes to lessening air pollution, natural gas cars get stellar ratings from the Environmental Protection Agency (EPA). On its air pollution scale, the EPA rates the Honda Civic GX 9.5 on a scale of 1 to 10.

In a gasoline engine atomized gasoline is set on fire by the sparkplug, producing a small "explosion." It is the expansion of the gasoline-air mixture in the combustion process that moves the piston to create motive force. In an NGV, the natural gas-air mixture is also fired by a sparkplug, and the expansion created moves the piston just as in a gasoline engine. The power production is very similar so that power can be channeled to the drive wheels using virtually identical technology.

The Pluses and Minuses of Natural Gas Vehicles

As we have seen, natural gas vehicles have many positives. They pollute much less than conventional gasoline cars. The technology is relatively simple and relatively inexpensive. And supplies of natural gas are large, both in the United States and abroad.

The downsides are less obvious but very important. To be carried in sufficient quantity to make the vehicles practical, natural gas has to be compressed. Compressed natural gas (CNG) is stored under pressure (about 3,000 pounds per square inch), so the container must be much stronger than a gasoline tank, which means it is heavier and more expensive. The special construction of the tanks makes NGVs more expensive to manufacture and that cost is ultimately passed on to consumers.

Potholes

In the early years of the automobile, gasoline was sold in hardware stores. It wasn't until two decades after the invention of the auto that gas stations became common. Some believe it will take that long for a natural gas infrastructure to be developed.

Equally important, there is just a tiny CNG infrastructure available to service natural gas vehicles in comparison to the vast gas-station-on-every-corner-where-there-isn't-a-Starbucks infrastructure built more than 100-plus years ago to service gasoline-powered vehicles.

This lack of infrastructure, not engine technology, is the major issue that has stood in the way of increased popularity of natural gas vehicles. Because of the lack of NGV refueling stations, the most practical way to refuel a natural gas car is to install a refueling system in your home, tapping into the natural gas line that provides your cooking and heating fuel. That requires an appliance, called Phill, which can cost more than $1,000, though promotions and tax credits might pay for much of that cost.

Potholes

There are an estimated 175,000 gas stations in the United States. In contrast there are only 1,350 or so CNG and LNG refueling stations, many of which are designed only to service trucks and buses, not common consumers.

Although spending money to set up a filling station for your vehicle in your own home might seem daunting, it is even more difficult for those of us who don't live in houses with a natural gas line or, for that matter, don't live in houses at all. Folks who live in apartments or mobile homes aren't precluded from owning natural gas vehicles, but they will frankly discover the going tough. Finding consumer-accessible sources of natural gas for vehicles is very difficult in most areas, and because sources of supply are limited, vendors can charge premium prices for the fuel.

But what about gas barbecue grills, you might ask. Isn't fuel available for them? Because so many gas grills are now in use, an infrastructure has sprung up to provide propane which is the primary barbecue grill fuel. Many gasoline stations offer the ability to refill gas-grill tanks, and others offer tank exchange programs. Unfortunately, vehicles calibrated to run on natural gas cannot run on propane or its close cousin, liquid petroleum gas (LPG), which is a mix of propane and butane. Propane and LPG are widely used in rural areas as heating and cooking fuels, and they can be used to power cars but currently are rarely used for that purpose.

Driving a Natural Gas Vehicle Day-to-Day

From behind the wheel, driving an NGV feels similar to driving a conventional gasoline car. It handles and steers in exactly the same manner as the car you own right now. Because natural gas isn't quite as punchy in providing power as gasoline, it might not accelerate quite as briskly, but most drivers won't even notice the difference.

Safety

It might seem dangerous to be driving around with a cylinder of highly explosive gas in your car, but remember you are currently driving around with a tank of highly flammable and potentially explosive liquid. Although there might be special circumstances in which NGVs are more dangerous than their gasoline counterparts, such as when the tank is punctured, those instances are extremely rare. Otherwise, an NGV is just as safe as a conventional car.

Some might be fearful of making natural gas fill-ups in their garage, but the currently available system makes the actual danger quotient very low. The upside is that the use of an at-home Phill fuel appliance means no more trips to the gasoline station ever.

Of course, safety is only part of the issue when it comes to insurance. Other factors include cost to repair and specialized parts. Because

NGVs do have unique components and are somewhat more costly to repair, insurance rates for NGVs are slightly (5 to 10 percent) higher than the rates for conventional vehicles of the same make and model.

Reliability

When it comes to longevity and reliability, the fact that natural gas cars are similar to their gasoline-powered cousins means NGVs will mimic similar conventional cars in their longevity and their resistance to failure. As with today's fuel-injected gasoline engines that often can go 100,000 miles before the spark plugs need changing, NGVs offer very low maintenance.

Because natural gas burns cleanly, there are fewer by-products from the combustion process that can blow by the piston rings and contaminate the oil. They require no gasoline filters, of course, so no filter changes are required, and although fuel-injected gasoline engines sometimes have problems associated with clogged injectors, natural gas eliminates that issue. The only bit of special attention they require is keeping an eye on the compressed natural gas fuel tank to make certain it is holding pressure. Well-maintained natural gas vehicles should offer more than 100,000 miles of trouble-free service.

Cost to Repair

Unlike hybrids that require expensive battery packs, NGVs don't feature anything that isn't very conventional with the exception of the fuel system. That implies they should be easy and inexpensive to get repaired. Sadly, that's not necessarily so.

Because of unfamiliarity with NGVs, not every mechanic will want to put his head under the hood of a natural gas vehicle, even if what he finds isn't too different from what he is used to. In fact, the biggest problem with getting an NGV repaired is finding someone willing to work on one. Currently, dealerships that sell natural gas vehicles are best suited to do repair work on them, and there is little competition for that business among independent shops. In light of that, repairs will be more expensive than repairs to conventional gasoline cars even though the technology is very similar. A typical service station mechanic could service an NGV; it is just doubtful he will want to. And specialists will charge more.

Cost to Operate

When you own a natural gas vehicle, its cost of operation can be a boon … if you don't take it cross-country very often. Using the cheapest fuel source—filling your fuel tank at home using your in-home source of natural gas—the cost of fuel is surprisingly low. On a gallon-of-gasoline-equivalency basis the cost of natural gas fuel is about half that of gasoline. In these days of expensive fuel prices, you can't do much better.

Natural gas is not quite as potent a source of energy as gasoline, which means you need to use more of it to power your vehicle, but in terms of fuel economy the EPA reports most natural gas vehicles deliver miles-per-gallon figures only slightly lower than those of similar gasoline cars. One thing this means is natural gas vehicles don't offer the startlingly high fuel economy figures that hybrids do. For instance, the natural gas Honda Civic GX has EPA fuel mileage numbers of 28 miles per gallon in the city and 39 miles per gallon on the highway with a combined figure of 32 mpg. In comparison, the very similar Honda Civic Hybrid has EPA fuel mileage numbers of 49 city/51 highway with a 50 mpg combined rating.

You might infer from this that the typical natural gas car will cost much more to drive than a hybrid, but the dollars-and-cents are actually on NGVs' side. Natural gas vehicles' lower fuel economy is more than offset by the lower cost of the fuel even when compared to a hybrid. Compared to a conventional gasoline-powered car, an NGV can deliver the same number of miles for about half the fuel cost.

Purchase Price

The few natural gas vehicles currently on the market are priced much higher than their conventional gasoline counterparts. For example, as this is being written the Honda Civic GX NGV vehicle has a suggested retail price of more than 25 percent of the equivalent gasoline-powered Honda Civic EX and 12 percent more than the Honda Civic Hybrid.

In addition, you will most likely want to pay for the Phill home refueling appliance if you have natural gas service at home, and that will set you back more than $1,000 (until you get rebates). So acquiring an NGV for your household has significant setup costs.

Projected Real Savings During the Ownership Cycle

The key to determining if a natural gas vehicle can "pencil" for you is both simple and profound. The simple revolves around some basic math and estimations of how and how much you drive. The profound revolves around how you value lower exhaust emissions, contributions to the environment, and a lessened reliance on foreign sources of fuel.

Figuring Your Ownership Cycle

To see if an NGV makes basic economic sense, you must put in place the vehicle ownership cost parameters we outlined in Chapter 4. To repeat, first determine how much you are paying for the vehicle and how much you expect it to be worth when you are ready to sell it. Second, determine how many miles a year you will drive. Third, estimate how much natural gas and gasoline will cost during your ownership period.

Are There Real Savings?

Because none of us can predict the future, we cannot say for certain if a natural gas vehicle will make economic sense or not with a strong degree of certainty. But each of us can make rationale assumptions to help us come up with testable hypotheses.

To make our example relatively simple, let's assume that the resale value of the NGV and the gasoline car will be the same at the end of the five-year ownership period. Let's further assume that you will drive either car 12,000 miles a year or 60,000 miles after 5 years. Finally, let's assume $3-a-gallon gasoline for the 5-year period and $1.50-a-gallon natural gas price. The EPA mileage for both the NGV and equivalent gasoline car is 30 mpg combined, a fair assumption.

That makes the cost-benefit analysis decently simple. Based on our assumptions, you will burn 2,000 gallons of gasoline to travel your 60,000 miles, and at $3 a gallon that will cost you $6,000. Or if you buy the natural gas vehicle, you will burn 2,000 gallons of $1.50-a-gallon natural gas, costing you $3,000 to go the same distance.

If the purchase cost were equal, you'd be three grand ahead in the NGV. But these days the purchase cost is not equal. Instead, the NGV commands a 25 percent premium. Figuring in the purchase price premium, that $3,000 advantage during your ownership period has just become a $2,000 loss.

But all is not lost. These days—and this can change with the whims of Congress—there is a $4,000 Federal tax credit that can offset much of the car's higher purchase price. In addition, there are also tax credits and incentives that can help pay for the Phill at-home fueling appliance. This means the NGV might well present almost immediate cost savings.

Although the illustrated example shows an NGV to be an on-paper loser pre-tax-credit, things change radically if you assume $4-a-gallon gasoline and $1-a-gallon equivalency natural gas. With these assumptions the gasoline car will burn $8,000 in fuel in a typical 5-year owner-ship period, and the NGV burns just $2,000. Even after paying a 25 percent premium for the NGV higher than the gasoline car, you're $1,000 ahead. And if there ,is a contnuing tax credit you'll be up still further.

> **Potholes**
>
> It would be nice to consider vehicles on their merits without worrying about government energy policy and tax credits, but that would be naïve. Although the oil and ethanol lobbies are strong, political proponents of NGVs are much harder to find, which means natural gas as vehicle fuel might be hard to find, too.

Who Benefits?

Individual circumstances vary so there is no one-size-fits-all answer to the question "Should I buy a natural gas vehicle?" We recommend strongly that you take a long, hard look at how much you drive, where you drive, and how long you drive, because you can't come to a good answer to that question without first looking at those parameters. You should also assess what value you put in driving a cleaner, greener vehicle and one that contributes to limiting our country's reliance on foreign oil.

> **Boosters**
>
> Don't minimize the benefit of driving in the carpool lane. If using the high-occupancy vehicle lane saves you a half hour a day, as it can in many urban areas, it will add up to 130 hours in productive time gained per year—the equivalent of a three-week vacation.

When you look at the dollars and cents, an individual with a long commute is the prime candidate for owning a natural gas vehicle. Such a person can fill her or his tank at home every night if necessary, so the worry about lack of fueling stations becomes moot. The longer the commute the more the savings, because natural gas is so much cheaper than gasoline on a power-equivalency basis. An added benefit to commuters is the fact that in some locales NGVs qualify for use in the carpool lane even with just one person aboard.

Who won't gain benefit from a natural gas vehicle? Well, if you do a great deal of long-distance driving, you might want to think twice about buying a natural gas vehicle. The same holds true if you don't live in a home with a natural gas connection, unless you have identified a convenient and cost-effective source for natural gas fill-up.

Guide to Currently Available Models

A guide to the currently available vehicles is relatively simple. Right now there is only one, the Honda Civic GX.

Honda Civic GX

The most recent version of the Honda Civic is one of the most honored cars in history. Among the awards it has captured are North American Car of the Year, *Motor Trend* magazine's Car of the Year, and *Kelley*

Blue Book's Best Redesigned Car of the Year. The natural gas-powered Honda GX offers everything the conventional Civic does and adds clean, inexpensive natural gas power.

Its 113-horsepower four-cylinder engine offers good acceleration and decent range. With an 8-gallon fuel cylinder, the DOE says the Civic GX will be able to travel approximately 200 miles on a full tank. This is less than a typical gasoline car, but it is balanced by the fact you can fill up every night if you use the at-home appliance.

Its EPA-projected fuel economy numbers are the same as for its gasoline-powered counterpart—28 miles per gallon city and 39 miles per gallon highway. Although that isn't as startling as the numbers for the Honda Civic Hybrid, with a fuel cost at about half that of a conventional gasoline-powered version, that means considerable savings.

The Least You Need to Know

- Natural gas burns very clean, curtailing exhaust emissions by significant percentages.
- You will pay more for a natural gas vehicle than for an equivalent gasoline vehicle.
- Refueling stations for natural gas vehicles are very limited.
- With the proper appliance, you can refuel your natural gas vehicle at home at significant savings.

7

Clean Diesel and Biodiesel Vehicles

In This Chapter

◆ Getting past the smell

◆ Learning the not-too-picky technology

◆ Cleaning up its act

◆ Putting the knock on NOX

They're smelly. They're dirty. They're noisy. And they're slow. That is how many Americans feel about diesel-powered automobiles. Even though many Europeans swear by the economy and reliability of their diesels, Americans entertained only a brief flirtation with diesel-powered cars during the fuel crisis of the early '80s, and that romance turned disastrous. American manufacturers converted some of their gasoline engines to diesel. Those engines failed right and left, leaving a bitter taste with many consumers. With this as background, you might be amazed to learn that many experts and at least a handful of vehicle manufacturers believe diesels are poised for a comeback in America.

Not only that, but future diesels will provide excellent fuel economy and remain environmentally clean.

The promise of excellent fuel economy from diesel engines is one of the great, if largely unreported, facts demonstrated by recent government and automaker research. When one looks at the nation's fuel economy champs as identified by the Environmental Protection Agency (EPA), several hybrids lead the pack but closely bunched right behind are diesel-powered models.

The Diesel Technology Forum claims diesels can reduce fuel consumption by 30 to 60 percent in some automotive models, obviously a giant reduction that has to be examined yet again in this age of onerous fuel prices. Further, those kinds of reductions can be accomplished with environmentally clean engines fitted with advanced exhaust emissions controls and after-treatment technology. That point of view was recently reinforced by a study by the National Academy of Sciences.

Although the combustion within a diesel engine might never be quite as clean as an internal combustion engine burning compressed natural gas or even gasoline, catalysts and filters can make the exhaust emissions almost as pure. The keys to clean diesel's low emissions are in both the combustion process itself, which can be made more precise and complete using computerized controls and sensors, and in the treatment and capture of exhaust emissions after the combustion process.

There is no doubt as to the fuel efficiency of diesel engines and now there is evidence that they can operate without producing the soot and stink they were once noted for. A lingering question regarding diesels comes from the fact that diesel fuel is made from petroleum. But the good news is it doesn't have to be. Biodiesel is a cleaner burning, renewable alternative fuel that can be made from any fat or vegetable oil, such as soybean oil. For instance, proponents of biodiesel say the market surplus in soybean oil from one bushel of soybeans makes 1.4 gallons of biodiesel, offering a lucrative new market for America's farmers without detracting from the nation's food supply.

When you add to that the anti-pollution and fuel efficiency of the new Common Rail Diesel (CRD) engine technology, you have a potent one-two punch that can benefit the nation if—and it's a big if—consumers can be convinced to give the new clean diesel/biodiesel technology a try.

What Is Diesel?

Although gasoline, ethanol, and natural gas are fuels, diesel is properly regarded as a method of combusting fuel to produce power. Because of the brilliant simplicity of Rudolf Diesel's creation, the diesel engine can burn a wide variety of fuels including crude oil, vegetable oils, animal fats, and even coal dust. It is frankly none-to-particular about what it burns, although it doesn't do well with highly volatile substances (such as gasoline or alcohol, for instance) because they will explode in the combustion chamber rather than burn. The in-cylinder explosions can damage the machinery, so diesel engineers avoid those fuels.

The key benefit of the diesel process is its high efficiency. By using a much higher compression ratio than a conventional gasoline engine (which uses the Otto cycle), the diesel engine is able to extract more power from the same amount of fuel. In addition, diesel fuel is typically more power-laden (by 15 percent or so) than gasoline. The combination results in more bang for your buck. There is some disagreement as to just how much more efficient diesels are than gasoline engines, but the general consensus is that they are, at the very least, 20 percent more efficient and perhaps as much as 50 percent more efficient in typical applications.

> **Boosters**
>
> Rudolf Diesel had a great idea but battles to protect the patents on his invention led to large debts, and he ended up committing suicide. Two decades after his death German technicians at Bosch turned his idea into a practical automobile engine.

What Are Clean Diesel Vehicles?

The problem that first bedeviled Rudolf Diesel in 1890 is the same problem that has prevented diesel engines from cleaning up their acts through the more than 100 years since—how do you inject fuel into the combustion chamber in the proper amount to get sufficient power while at the same time promoting clean burning? Frankly, up until the 1980s diesel engineers were more interested in getting power and longevity than in getting clean exhaust, which helps explain diesel's reputation for producing smoke and stink. But now the emphasis has changed, and there has been a big breakthrough.

The breakthrough is the common-rail injection system (CRIS), and diesels that use it are commonly called CRDs. The beauty of the common-rail fuel system is that it maintains high injection pressures independent of engine speed, which allows it to much more precisely inject small amounts of fuel into the combustion chamber at the exact right moment. Because of its precision, the result is maximum power with a minimum of exhaust emissions. The soot and smoke that we used to associate with diesels are a thing of the past with common-rail technology. Often common-rail systems are teamed with turbocharging that uses the flow of exhaust gases to compress the air going into the combustion chamber before ignition for even more efficiency. Large over-the-road diesel trucks have been using turbocharging for years.

How Do Clean Diesel Vehicles Work?

Even with CRIS, diesels are not as clean-running as gasoline engines, especially in the emissions of particulates and nitrogen oxides. And after many years of experimentation, engineers on both sides of the Atlantic came to the conclusion that trying to refine the combustion process still further was not going to bring acceptable results. So as they have with catalytic converters on gasoline engines, they turned to cleaning the exhaust emissions after the combustion process.

The particulate problem was largely solved by the introduction of the maintenance-free particulate filter, pioneered by Mercedes-Benz and now offered as standard equipment in all diesel passenger cars in many countries.

Boosters

While the Europeans focus on CO_2 emissions and lowering fuel consumption, legislation in the United States is geared primarily toward achieving extremely low NOX emissions.

Nitrogen oxides (NOX) were another story. NOX is problematic for several reasons. Above a certain concentration nitrous oxides can irritate the human respiratory system. They also damage plant life by causing acid rain, and they contribute to the accumulation of ozone. In the presence of sunlight, this results in smog. That's why there are limits on NOX emissions in effect all over the world, and they are becoming more and more stringent. The strictest limits are in the United States, with California playing a pioneering role in these efforts.

Having come to the conclusion that some sort of exhaust treatment is necessary to conform to government standards for NOX emissions, engineers have put into place several systems with a common theme—a catalytic converter designed to reduce NOX emissions heavily. For example, the system in a recent Ford Focus concept vehicle has a catalyst that uses a water solution of urea sprayed on the catalyst to remove NOX from the exhaust. To ensure that urea is always added to the vehicle, a process called "co-fueling" is employed. Co-fueling fills the diesel and urea tanks at the same time, so the operation is seamless for the customer.

The Mercedes-Benz BLUETEC system for passenger cars includes an oxidizing catalytic converter and a particulate filter. BLUETEC vehicles then add one of two additional technologies for reducing nitrogen-oxide emissions. The first is an improved nitrogen oxide storage catalytic converter and the second is a selected catalytic reduction (SCR) catalytic converter with "AdBlue" injection. Although either method is effective enough to allow the vehicles that use it to achieve 50-state certification, the SCR catalytic converter with AdBlue injection is particularly advantageous. By injecting an aqueous reducing agent into the exhaust gas flow, it lowers emissions of nitrogen oxides by as much as 80 percent, which makes it the most effective exhaust gas treatment method for diesel engines.

What Is Biodiesel?

Biodiesel is a catchall term that refers to diesel fuels that are derived from biological sources such as plants and animals instead of petroleum. (In fact, the original source of petroleum might also be plants or animals, but because that is still under debate and because that process happened thousands if not millions of years ago, let's stick to the commonly held meaning of the term.) Chemically, biodiesel is somewhat different in composition from conventional diesel fuel (sometimes referred to as "petrodiesel"), but as we have seen, diesel engines aren't too hard to please when it comes to the fuels they use.

Key advantages to biodiesel versus petrodiesel fuels are huge. First, of course, biodiesel is made from nonfossil based products, so it is renewable and it can help us limit our reliance on foreign sources of petroleum. In fact, it can be made from products that are now considered waste and are simply disposed of, which makes it even more efficient for the overall ecosystem in which we live. Biodiesel is also nontoxic and biodegradable. Another benefit is that biodiesel can be mixed with petrodiesel to increase the *lubricity* of *ultra-low sulfur diesel*. Although, because biodiesel can contain sulfur itself, care must be taken that it doesn't send the mix over the 15 parts per million bogey that defines the fuel. Used in a mix with petrodiesel, biodiesel can both extend our fossil fuel supply and result in cleaner exhaust emissions. Helping us use waste in a productive manner is icing on the cake.

Definitions _____

Lubricity is the measure of the ability of a liquid introduced between two surfaces to limit friction and wear.

Ultra-low sulfur diesel is diesel fuel that contains far less of the potentially hazardous substance sulfur than do typical American diesel fuels. Sulfur is not only a pollutant, but it can foul and clog catalytic converters and particulate filters meant to deal with other pollutants.

How Does Biodiesel Work?

The very good news is that biodiesel fuels work well in virtually any diesel engine capacity, particularly in passenger cars and trucks. Although the chemical composition of biodiesel is somewhat different from conventional diesel fuel, it offers combustion properties that are very similar, including, very importantly, the amount of stored energy it packs per ounce and its *cetane number.*

Definitions _____

The **cetane number** or cetane rating is the measure of combustibility under pressure used as a relative measure to rank diesel fuels.

There are a couple of issues to be dealt with when using biodiesel, however. First, some types of biodiesel have a higher-temperature gel point (the point where they begin to solidify similar to Jell-O in a refrigerator) than conventional diesel fuel. This could lead to cold-weather starting problems because of lack of fuel flow, but it doesn't seem to be a major problem. And it can be addressed by the addition of a fuel heater, if necessary. Another more vexing problem is the solvent qualities of biodiesel. Introduced into an engine that has been using conventional diesel fuel, the solvent action of the biodiesel fuel can loosen deposits and "gunk" and lead to fuel filter and fuel injector clogs.

Although there are a few problems, the important thing to note is that the potential downsides are few and easily addressed while the upsides of using biodiesel are many. Undoubtedly the best-case scenario from a clean-air point of view is the use of biodiesel in clean diesel engines that use modern features such as common-rail fuel injection technology and stringent exhaust treatment steps such as particulate filters and urea-injection catalytic converters. This combination of new technology and biologically based fuels can be labeled "new diesels."

The Pluses and Minuses of "New Diesel" Vehicles

The key advantages new diesels offer are improved greenhouse gas emissions and potentially lower overall fuel costs based on the fact that diesel engines are inherently more efficient than gasoline engines. It should be noted that in terms of what are best termed more traditional pollution-causing emissions, including carbon monoxide, nitrous oxides, and particulates, clean diesel technology combined with the use of conventional diesel fuel simply equals the best conventional gasoline engine performance in the area. But when used in combination with biodiesel, the EPA says that 100 percent biodiesel will reduce carbon dioxide greenhouse gas emissions by 75 percent. Using a blend of 20 percent biodiesel mixed with 80 percent petrodiesel (so-called B20) will reduce CO_2 emissions by 15 percent. Biodiesel in concert with clean diesel technology also reduces particulates, sulfur dioxide, and carbon monoxide. Because biodiesel is made from renewable resources and even waste products, it has the potential to limit our reliance on foreign sources of energy, and at the same time it can foster the cleanup of our present environment by encouraging the recycling of what is otherwise considered garbage.

The potential for lower overall fuel costs comes from two factors. First and foremost is the fact that diesel engines are inherently more efficient than gasoline engines. When used in a mid-size sedan such as the Volkswagen Jetta, for example, the turbodiesel engine achieves EPA highway fuel economy 35 percent better than the similar gasoline-powered model and city fuel economy that is 40 percent better. (In fairness, though, the turbodiesel model is less powerful and a trifle slower than the gasoline version.) The other potential savings can occur because diesel has the potential to be less expensive than gasoline, especially if biodiesel can be used to supplement expensive petrodiesel. But as of now, that is a big if. Currently diesel fuel prices are closely aligned to gasoline prices, which makes sense because they are both derived from crude oil.

As you surely know, diesel-powered cars and light trucks have been around for a long time. But diesel's reputation as noisy, stinky, and sooty (who are not, by the way, Donald Duck's nephews) has limited diesel's appeal to the mainstream American car buyer. These days in the United States, it takes a rugged individualist to buy a diesel car, and the proof of that is the fact that diesel-powered passenger vehicles represent about a quarter of 1 percent of the overall vehicle fleet (0.27 percent).

The picture is completely different in Europe. Clean diesel engines already account for about one third of all vehicles on the road there. In some European countries, spurred by tax laws that favor diesels because of their lower fuel consumption, clean diesel cars represent 60 percent of new-car sales.

While European regulations have favored diesels, U.S. regulations have done just the opposite. In fact, California clean air rules that also are followed by New York and several New England states have been so hard on diesels that they have essentially prevented them from being sold in those states. The two culprits cited by the California Air Resources Board (CARB) are particulates, which it cites as carcinogenic, and nitrogen oxides, which can cause smog. Although particulate filters can address the particulate problem and special catalysts can address NOX, CARB hasn't had much enthusiasm for either, because there are questions about maintaining their abilities to keep working through the life of the vehicle. This has been exacerbated by the high sulfur content in conventional diesel fuel, because sulfur can render particulate filters useless.

In a move that is expected to spur diesel sales in the United States, the composition of diesel fuel has been changed to a "low-sulfur" formulation. Companies such as Mercedes-Benz and Volkswagen have been big proponents of diesel vehicles and feel that this will open the floodgates of interest in diesel. Other companies such as Ford and Honda also are responding to the fuel regulations with vehicles set to go that meet the new, more stringent exhaust emission standards and can take advantage of the low-sulfur fuel. Still there is some resistance from regulators because the emissions control systems on even the cleanest of clean diesel engines will not function without maintenance for the life of the vehicle.

The most important maintenance procedure in the loop is the requirement to add a solution to the catalytic system that controls NOX emissions. If the tank runs dry, the engine will spit out a much larger amount of NOX. Ford proposes to handle this issue by linking the addition of the urea solution to the fueling procedure, but there is no general agreement on this yet. And for diesels to really win the blessings of regulators across the country, something needs to be done on this score.

> **Potholes**
>
> The EPA seems open to clean diesel technology, but currently available models don't score well on its rating system. For example, the Jeep Liberty diesel gets a 1 on the 1 to 10 air pollution scale.

The final issue regarding diesels could be a plus or a minus depending on whether you're a "half-full" or "half-empty" kind of person. Currently, diesel fuel is not nearly as accessible as is gasoline to most buyers. And that factor is multiplied 100 times over if you seek biodiesel instead of conventional petrodiesel. But the encouraging news is that low-sulfur diesel has been mandated by the government, so it will soon be the dominant available diesel fuel. And low-sulfur diesel, biodiesel and petrobiodiesel mixes such as B20, can use the same "gas station" infrastructure that is already in place.

Driving a Clean Diesel Vehicle Day-to-Day

When you get behind the wheel of a modern clean diesel car, you have a driving experience that mimics that of a conventional gasoline car. In the past, diesels had slow-heating glowplugs that made you wait several seconds before you could start the engine, but that is a thing of the past. Power, handling, and ride are all very comparable to gasoline cars. One slight difference is that diesel engines are better at creating torque, which simply described is "pulling power," than they are at creating peak horsepower. Because of this, diesel engines' horsepower numbers are a bit misleading, because in around-town driving and acceleration on a freeway on-ramp, for example, torque is a more important factor than horsepower. Another positive factor regarding diesel models is their range on a tank of fuel. Because the engines are more efficient than gasoline engines and the fuel tanks for both diesel and gasoline versions of the same car are similar in size, diesel vehicles offer more miles between fill-ups.

Boosters

BMW, Mercedes-Benz, and Volkswagen are so high on "clean diesel" technology that they recently announced that they would work together to promote the technology in the United States under the name BLUETEC.

Safety

On the safety front, diesels have no great safety advantages or disadvantages in comparison to conventional vehicles. One small safety advantage is that diesel fuel is less flammable than gasoline, so it is less likely to burn or even explode in an accident. Generally, diesel's safety performance is comparable to similar gasoline-powered models from the same manufacturer.

On the insurance front, the only factor that points to a difference in rates for diesels and gasoline cars is that diesel engines are more expensive to build and thus to replace than gasoline engines. But the difference is not enough to affect rates much. Further, diesel drivers generally have better-than-average driving records, which mitigates the engine expense liability.

Reliability

In addition to the reputation as stinky and sooty, diesels have another, much more positive reputation, and that is longevity. Diesel engines, when properly maintained, last a long, long time. One reason is their very stout construction. Another reason is the fact that there is not as much that can go wrong. There is no conventional ignition system so there are no sparkplugs, sparkplug wires, or ignition module that could fail. An owner of a new clean-diesel vehicle can reasonably expect a minimum of 100,000 miles of trouble-free service from his or her properly maintained vehicle.

When it comes to maintenance there are just two things to remember. One, regular oil changes are more important to the health of a diesel engine than they are to a gasoline engine. Because of their higher compression ratios and the composition of their fuel, diesels deposit more soot in the crankcase than gasoline engines. For that reason, a top-quality oil that can suspend those particles is vital to avoiding excessive wear. And when that oil has reached the end of its useful life it should be changed promptly for the same reason.

The other factor is the maintenance of the exhaust emissions system. Although the particulate filter is generally good for the life of the car, the NOX catalyst might require the addition of a special solution. Without that solution, the vehicle's NOX output will be much greater.

Cost to Repair

Know any good diesel mechanics? Automobile diesel mechanics is a specialty, but the prevalence of light-, medium- and heavy-duty trucks that all use diesel engines means the skill isn't all that rare. Further, those manufacturers who are expected to put a push on diesel in the next few years—Mercedes-Benz, DaimlerChrysler, Ford, and Honda among them—will do a good job of training technicians to maintain and fix diesel vehicles. Even though you won't find a qualified diesel mechanic in every corner gas station, getting your diesel-powered vehicle serviced should be neither a problem nor a huge expense.

Diesels also benefit from the fact that their technology is rather simple. For instance, they don't use conventional sparkplugs or ignition systems, so those items, of course, are absent from their service requirements. To be fair, today's gasoline cars often can go 100,000 miles before requiring a traditional tune-up.

Cost to Operate

If trends hold, the cost to operate a diesel vehicle should be lower than the cost to operate a comparable gasoline-powered vehicle. The key difference is in fuel costs. The other factors, depreciation, financing, insurance, maintenance, and repairs are essentially a wash, but in terms of fuel costs, the overall better efficiency of the diesel powerplant carries the day. For example, projected 5-year fuel costs for a gasoline-powered Volkswagen Golf are 28 percent higher than the projected 5-year fuel costs for the turbodiesel version of the same vehicle.

These projections are based on the assumptions that the relative prices of gasoline and diesel fuel will remain the same. If that relationship changes for some reason, all that could change. Further, these projections are based on the use of conventional "petrodiesel." If your desire is to use biodiesel, again, all bets are off. Depending on the source, biodiesel eventually could be less expensive and perhaps much less expensive than petrodiesel is now. But in the short term, biodiesel—such as E85—is priced at what the market will bear and/or at the whim of the individuals who offer it.

Purchase Price

Diesel-powered vehicles, both cars and trucks, generally command premium prices in the marketplace these days versus their gasoline-powered cousins. There are a couple of reasons for this. The first is the diesel's legendary reputation for longevity and toughness. Another is the fact that, given diesel's better efficiency, fuel costs are expected to be lower. And then there is the fact that for a select few consumers there is no substitute for diesel—it's a "gotta have it" proposition.

How big is that premium? For both cars and trucks it's in the neighborhood of 10 to 15 percent of the Manufacturer's Suggested Retail Price (MSRP). Even with somewhat higher purchase prices, however, projections indicate you will come out ahead of the gasoline-vehicle buyer at the conclusion of the typical 5-year ownership period.

Projected Real Savings During the Ownership Cycle

Determining whether a clean diesel vehicle will "pencil" for you is much simpler than the procedure for vehicles that use other fuels, such as E85, because the relationship between the prices of gasoline and diesel are more easily projected. Of course, as commodities, both prices are subject to change and both prices are subject to fuel interruptions because a large proportion of the fuels are derived from foreign-sourced petroleum. But putting in place a series of scenarios that depicts "what-if" possibilities does not require advanced physics or a grasp of the occult.

Figuring Your Ownership Cycle

To make a determination on the advisability of buying a diesel rather than a gasoline vehicle in your situation, you must put in place the vehicle ownership cost parameters we outlined in Chapter 4. First, determine how much you are paying for the vehicle and how much you expect it to be worth when you are ready to sell it. Second, determine how many miles a year you will drive. Third, estimate how much diesel fuel and gasoline will cost over your ownership period.

Are There Real Savings?

Let's test a hypothesis or two to see if buying a diesel will make economic sense for you in your situation. Remember, you can tailor these examples to your own expectations, but even if you don't, they will provide a good comparative look at the relative merits of each purchase.

In an effort to make the hypotheses relatively simple, let's assume that the resale value of the diesel and the equivalent gasoline car will be the same at the end of the 5-year ownership period. Let's further assume that you will drive either car 12,000 miles a year or 60,000 miles after 5 years. Finally, let's assume $3-a-gallon gasoline for the 5-year period and $3.25-a-gallon diesel fuel price. The EPA mileage for the diesel is 37 miles per gallon while the equivalent gasoline car gets 27 mpg combined.

That makes the cost analysis relatively easy to figure. Based on our assumptions, you will burn 2,222 gallons of gasoline to travel your 60,000 miles, and at $3 a gallon that will cost you $6,666. Or if you buy the diesel version of the vehicle, you will burn 1,621 gallons of $3.25-a-gallon diesel fuel, costing you $5,268 to rack up the same number of miles.

That gives a total fuel cost benefit to the diesel vehicle, but we're not done yet. Let us further assume that the purchase price of the diesel was $21,000 while the purchase price of the gasoline-powered version was $20,000. This reduces the diesel's $1,398 cost advantage to just $398.

As you realize, though, things change considerably if you make different assumptions. For the sake of argument, let's assume $4-a-gallon gasoline and $4-a-gallon diesel fuel, which is not beyond the realm of possibility. With these assumptions the gasoline car will burn up $8,888 in fuel in the typical 5-year ownership period, while the diesel will use just $6,484 in fuel. After figuring in the $1,000 purchase price premium, that represents a very nice $1,404 cost advantage for the diesel.

Who Benefits?

Because better fuel efficiency is a diesel engine's prime benefit, those who drive the most miles will save the most by owning a diesel. The justifiable reputation diesels have garnered for longevity, toughness, and simplicity just furthers this premise. After all, that's the reason truckers have long preferred diesels to gasoline-powered vehicles.

On the environmental side, there are few if any benefits. Manufacturers are now struggling to get diesel engines to conform to already established regulatory landmarks, and they are resorting to ever-more-exotic methods to get there. That doesn't mean that the real promise of the phrase "clean diesel" can't be realized, but in actual practice the available vehicles aren't there yet. The one environmental benefit that diesels do deliver is an overall decrease in greenhouse gas emissions, and that is accomplished simply by the fact that they burn less fuel to go a given distance.

Biodiesel does hold promise both in terms of further efficiencies and in the ability of diesel technology to lessen our reliance on foreign oil. But we are currently a long way from having biodiesel fuels available in large quantities for the masses.

Who won't see benefits from a diesel vehicle? If you drive fewer than 10,000 miles a year any economic benefit you'd gain from owning a diesel would be small at best, and you would have to deal with the hassle of finding diesel fuel.

Guide to Currently Available Models

A guide to the currently available vehicles includes a thumbnail description of each vehicle currently on the market that uses the gamut of clean diesel technology.

Mercedes-Benz E320 BLUETEC

Take the mainstay Mercedes-Benz E-Class sedan, add a clean diesel system and what have you got? A vehicle that feels similar to a conventional E-Class.

Mercedes-Benz GL320 BLUETEC

"Gas-guzzling" is a term that often precedes the letters SUV. By adding the efficient diesel system, the adjective gas-guzzler is a serious misnomer.

Ford Powerstroke Pickup

Pickup trucks have long been bastions of diesel engines. Now Ford has taken the step to make the best use of the new low-sulfur diesel fuel.

The Least You Need to Know

- ◆ Diesel engines are more fuel-efficient than gasoline engines.

- ◆ The diesel combustion process is "dirtier" than gasoline combustion in a conventional engine so extra equipment must be added to diesels to clean their exhaust to regulated levels.

- ◆ Biodiesel, diesel fuel made from renewable sources such as vegetable oil, holds promise on efficiency and environmental fronts but it is not ready for mass consumption yet.

- ◆ Diesel vehicles are generally more cost-effective than conventional vehicles even when taking into account the premium prices they command.

Chapter 8

New Tech Gasoline Vehicles

In This Chapter

- ◆ Evolving the gasoline engine
- ◆ Determining what a PZEV is
- ◆ Having two engines in one
- ◆ Being similar to conventional engines only better

The gasoline engine gets no respect. Throughout automotive history countless numbers of inventors, tinkerers, mechanics, and everyday folks like you and me have cursed it, vilified it, and castigated it. In many ways it is a cantankerous contraption with a plethora of pesky moving parts. It drinks precious fossil fuel and spews out noxious chemicals not to mention the non-noxious carbon dioxide that is the hobgoblin of current global warming. Advocates of other technologies—steam, electricity, diesel, natural gas, and so on—have tried to make the gasoline engine a quaint museum piece, gathering dust in a Greenfield Village-like recreation. Yet, for all its faults, the gasoline engine endures.

Even though "gas-guzzler" is a derogatory term that should correctly be leveled at the biggest and most fuel-thirsty of the gasoline engines on the market, it is easy to forget that today's hybrids use gasoline engines, too. True, the smaller, specially tuned gasoline engines in hybrids use less fuel than their big brothers to propel vehicles and help keep battery packs topped off. But even as the hybrids seem to promise an end to our addict-like reliance on foreign oil, they also demonstrate quite clearly that gasoline technology is not dead or even dying.

So despite the fact that the gasoline engine is being demonized, thousands of engineers and technicians around the world are laboring day and night to make this curmudgeonly power plant behave more civilly. The happy fact is that they have made and continue to make remarkable progress. Today's gasoline engines are a far cry from the sputtering, wheezing assemblages of Benz and Daimler. Today's most modern gasoline engines are very clean, very efficient, and very reliable. They start when you want them to start, run all day long with virtually no daily maintenance, and have life expectancies longer than many kennel-bred dogs. Yet to some, they are the enemy.

Even as many environmentalists have embraced hybrid vehicles for their pure electric cleanliness, they have conveniently overlooked the fact that they still burn fossil fuels and still create emissions. And the most vociferous of the environmentalists, who are acting with altruistic intents, are loath to settle for hybrids for just those reasons. Many of them are seeking a resurgence in the all-electric vehicles, overlooking that the electricity that powers them has to be generated somehow, and these days much of that is by coal- or natural gas-fired generating plants. And those plants emit chemicals, particulates, and carbon dioxide, too. There's just no way around that.

While hardcore environmentalists push for zero-emission vehicles, others suggest that, as tempting as a complete revolution in vehicular technology might be to protect this and future generations, an evolution in engine technology that allows us to make incremental gains without throwing away what is good and effective in our current vehicles is worthy of consideration. The fact is, whether it is commonly recognized or not, that evolution is going on day by day, spurred by public opinion, public policy, and the realities of the fossil fuel supply.

Evidence of the evolution of the gasoline engine abounds. Lighter materials, more sophisticated valve arrangements, and better fuel delivery systems mark the century-long development of the automotive gasoline engine. Spurred by Clean Air legislation and regulations that began in the 1960s, the gasoline engine has been made remarkably cleaner and more efficient during the last 50 years. The introduction of the catalytic converter and the precise air and fuel delivery that have been enabled by computer-controlled fuel injection have resulted in some remarkably "clean" gasoline engines.

As an example, look at the gasoline-powered vehicles that meet California's stringent Partial Zero Emission Vehicle standards, which are in effect not only in California, but also in New York, Massachusetts, Maine, and Vermont. First, such vehicles must have tailpipe emissions that meet the *Super Ultra Low Emission Vehicle (SULEV)* standards.

It must demonstrate "zero" gasoline *evaporative emissions,* virtually eliminating emissions from the vehicle's fuel system, and it also must provide warranty coverage to ensure that the vehicle will meet these stringent requirements for an extended lifetime of 15 years or 150,000 miles. As of this writing, more than 30 vehicle models qualify for the Partial Zero Emission Vehicle (PZEV) rating, and more are expected to reach this very high standard of performance.

? **Definitions** _____

Super Ultra Low Emission Vehicles (SULEWV), as defined by the California Air Resources Board, are 90 percent cleaner than the average new-model-year car, which means 90 percent cleaner than vehicles that meet the already stringent clean air standards administered by the federal government.

Evaporative emissions are gaseous discharges emanating from the fuel system and from the process of filling your gas tank. A vehicle with no evaporative emissions typically has fewer emissions while being driven than a typical gasoline car has while standing still.

As with hybrids, PZEVs typically deliver not only very low exhaust emissions but also better than average fuel economy, and they do this by combining several technologies that include highly sophisticated computerized fuel injection and engine management, advanced catalytic converters, and well-sealed fuel systems. This multiphased approach is similar to that of hybrids in that each system contributes to the overall positive effect.

Multi-Displacement Active Fuel Technology

In addition to PZEVs, another gasoline engine technology has recently gone into production that is designed to reduce fuel consumption, and it is being used on some of the largest, most fuel-thirsty vehicles on sale in the United States. Called variously Multi-Displacement System or Active Fuel Management, the system allows engines to operate in two separate modes—one with full cylinder operation and the other with partial cylinder operation. The industry catch-all term for the technology is displacement-on-demand (DoD).

> **Boosters**
>
> DaimlerChrysler has labeled its two-mode gasoline engine technology Multi-Displacement System (MDS), while General Motors calls its very similar system Active Fuel Management (AFM). The industry short-hand for the systems is "displacement on demand" because the engines can perform similar to large- or small-displacement engines depending on load.

An example of displacement on demand technology is the 5.7-liter HEMI V8 engine being used in a number of Chrysler Group vehicles, including the Chrysler 300C sedan, Dodge Magnum RT station wagon, and Jeep Grand Cherokee sport utility vehicle. Thanks to fully functional cylinder deactivation, the MDS engine seamlessly alternates between high-fuel-economy four-cylinder mode when less power is needed and eight-cylinder mode when more power is requested by the driver.

When a vehicle equipped with displacement on demand is in a situation that requires relatively modest power—for instance, cruising at 60 miles per hour (mph) on a level road—the system deactivates the valve lifters that normally actuate the valves in four of the engine's eight cylinders. This keeps the valves in those four cylinders closed, and there is no combustion in those cylinders as long as the engine senses it is lightly loaded. In addition to stopping combustion, which saves fuel, additional energy is retained because no air is pumped through the deactivated cylinders.

How Do Displacement on Demand Vehicles Work?

Cylinder deactivation has been tried since early in the automotive age. But most such systems, including the notorious Cadillac 4-6-8 system of the early 1980s, had difficulties during the transition phase. Those potential pitfalls have been overcome by the speed of electronic engine controls, the sophistication of the algorithms controlling the system, and the use of electronic rather than mechanical throttle control. The Chrysler HEMI can transition from eight-cylinder operation to four in 40 milliseconds (0.040 seconds).

Potholes

In response to the 1979 to 1980 fuel crisis, Cadillac introduced its 4-6-8 system that enabled its V8 engine to operate on four, six, or eight cylinders, but the technology was so problem-prone that it was quickly withdrawn from the market.

General Motors is using similar technology in its full-size Chevrolet Suburban, Chevrolet Tahoe, and GMC Yukon SUVs and its full-size Chevrolet Silverado and GMC Sierra pickup trucks. GM introduced the first V6 application of Active Fuel Management on the 3.9-liter V6 offered in the Chevrolet Impala. In the GM V6, the vehicle operates as a conventional V6-powered vehicle in heavy-load situations such as quick acceleration from a stop and hill-climbing, and it operates as a three-cylinder in light cruising.

So what does this mean in terms of improved fuel economy? The numbers generated are hardly the amazing gains hybrids offer, but they do represent solid, positive achievement. Chrysler has claimed that its customers experience estimated fuel economy gains of up to 20 percent under certain driving conditions, predominantly highway driving, and as much as a 10 percent aggregate improvement. General Motors suggests motorists might see similar gains in their large pickups and SUVs. Preliminary testing of the Chevy Impala equipped with the Active Fuel Management V6 indicated an estimated 20 mpg in the city and 29 mpg on the highway, improvements of approximately 5.5 percent and 7.5 percent, respectively.

Although some might scoff at these gains as miniscule, it is instructive to look at them in the context of the entire American vehicle fleet. Even though there are fewer than half a million hybrid vehicles on the road today, DaimlerChrysler has more than 1 million MDS vehicles in service in the United States, while General Motors claims it will have more than 2 million AFM vehicles in use by 2008. That means the displacement on demand technology could save 150 to 200 million gallons of gasoline a year by 2010.

Another important note on this technology: the improved fuel economy is realized without any change in driver experience or functionality. Displacement on demand vehicles offer power, response, cargo, and towing capabilities that are equal or better than vehicles equipped with conventional gasoline engines of the same displacement. Drivers will receive the benefits without changing their driving habits and without compromising style, comfort, or convenience.

No vehicle these days combines a PZEV rating with the use of displacement on demand technology. That is due largely to the fact that it is easier for a small car equipped with a relatively small engine to achieve PZEV status, and displacement on demand technology is being applied to vehicles that can most benefit from its abilities; namely, large pickups, sedans, and SUVs. But we can lump these two advanced vehicle types under the heading "New Tech Gasoline Engine Vehicles" because they exhibit similar characteristics in the hands of their owners.

The Pluses and Minuses of New Tech Gasoline Engine Vehicles

These new tech vehicles are an evolution in transportation rather than a revolution. They won't change the world in the same way a sudden wholesale switch to electrics or even hybrids would. You could say they are the same, but better, than the gasoline cars we have now.

With PZEVs the major difference between them and other similar vehicles that don't achieve a PZEV rating is the amount of emissions they expel. In terms of fuel economy their performance is very similar to like-size non-PZEV vehicles and it is generally very good because the vehicles are relatively small. For example, a PZEV Ford Focus and its non-PZEV brother achieve identical Environmental Protection Agency (EPA) mileage ratings of 27 mpg city/37 mph highway. However, on the EPA's Air Pollution scale (1 to 10, with 10 being best) the PZEV Focus scores a 9.5 while the non-PZEV Focus is rated just an 8. This is representative of other PZEVs versus non-PZEVs.

For engines that use Multi-Displacement System or Active Fuel Management technology, the key difference is in fuel economy. The overall improvement on the EPA city/highway cycles is somewhere between 5 and 10 percent, depending on application.

The best news for both of these technologies is that there are no real downsides. Though they do cost somewhat more to produce than conventional gasoline-powered vehicles, the purchase prices to the consumers are generally very similar to those of similar vehicles that lack the technology. An additional plus for some AFM-equipped vehicles from General Motors is that they are also Flex Fuel-capable, which could have some benefits especially if ethanol is low-priced in your area.

> **Boosters**
>
> A 5 percent improvement in EPA mileage pales in comparison to the double-digit gains offered by the hybrids. But such a gain can help significantly in reducing gasoline consumption, because sales of vehicles with such engines have been and are expected to be brisk.

Driving a New Tech Gasoline Vehicle Day-to-Day

One of the key advantages of driving a new tech gasoline vehicle is that it mimics the performance of a conventional gasoline vehicle.

It accelerates, stops, handles, and tows just as a typical vehicle in its class. The key difference with a Partial Zero Emission Vehicle is the extremely low exhaust and evaporative emissions it produces versus a standard car. The key difference with a displacement on demand vehicle is the 5 to 10 percent better fuel economy than similar conventionally powered vehicles. Of course, all these vehicles use gasoline as their power source, so you can make use of the gasoline infrastructure for refueling.

Safety

When it comes to safety, vehicles powered by new tech gasoline engines offer the same performance as the conventionally powered vehicles from the same manufacturer. The technologies are essentially safety-neutral. They provide no more safety and no more risks than conventional vehicles. Because many of the new tech engines are installed in more recently designed chassis, they likely will be equipped with more modern safety equipment—side curtain airbags, rollover mitigation systems, and electronic stability control, for example—but over time, as the technologies become more prevalent, this will be less and less a factor.

On the insurance front, new tech vehicles are so similar to conventional cars in all the ways that matter to insurance carriers that rates for conventional cars apply. They present no special hazards, and though they do use special parts, they are not markedly more expensive than similar conventional parts.

Reliability

The reliability of PZEVs is very similar to that of the conventional versions of the same models. Because a variety of auto manufacturers build PZEV vehicles, the quality of the design and manufacture varies, but there have been no reports that PZEVs are more prone to require repair than are conventional vehicles. The big plus in favor of the technology is that key components in their drivetrain are warrantied for 15 years or 150,000 miles. It is logical to expect 100,000 miles of trouble-free service from a properly maintained PZEV vehicle.

As to those vehicles that use displacement on demand systems, the jury is still out. Previous attempts at multi-displacement engines have been nothing short of disastrous. However, early indications are that this time around the manufacturers have designed and developed these engines for superior longevity. Both General Motors and Chrysler have put literally millions of development miles and simulated miles on engines using the systems. Further, the displacement on demand engines are covered by lengthy warranties that extend across the typical ownership period. On the other hand, these engines have not been in consumers' hands long enough for us to know whether displacement on demand is bulletproof technology.

Cost to Repair

Though they differ from one another, PZEV and displacement on demand vehicles are so similar to their conventional gasoline-powered siblings that the cost-to-repair reflects conventional engine rates. In a PZEV the key mechanical differences are in the fuel system and post-combustion treatment area (largely catalytic converters). These systems are more expensive than those in conventional cars but they carry the 15-year/150,000 warranty. In a displacement on demand vehicle, the differences lie in the *valvetrain* and the electronic engine controls.

Generally, electronic engine controls either work or they don't. There is little middle ground, and the failure rate is very low. The altered valvetrain is more complicated than a typical conventional engine, but indications are that the changes are robustly engineered. If an MDS or AFM system does fail, however, it will be more expensive to fix than a conventional engine.

> **?** **Definitions** ___
>
> An engine's **valvetrain** is the collection of valves and their associated mechanical and hydraulic operating mechanisms that allow an internal combustion engine to ingest air and expel exhaust gases.

Due to their unfamiliarity with displacement on demand engines, some mechanics might shy away from repairing a valvetrain malfunction, but that scenario should be rare.

Cost to Operate

Partial Zero Emission Vehicles cost less to operate than the average conventional car, but only because they are smaller than the average conventional car and are powered by relatively smaller engines. Compared to cars of similar size and power that use gasoline engines, the cost to operate will be virtually the same.

Displacement on demand vehicles present a different picture. Their major benefit is better fuel economy, so they will be somewhat less expensive to operate than conventional vehicles sporting engines with the same power potential. The cost savings won't be startling, however, probably around 5 to 10 percent less.

Purchase Price

Even though PZEVs and displacement on demand vehicles do cost more than similar conventionally powered vehicles to build, that difference is not nearly on the scale of the hybrid-conventional vehicle differential. In fact AFM- and MDS-equipped vehicles are being offered at virtually the same prices as vehicles without the technology. An added plus is some displacement on demand powertrains are also Flex Fuel-capable, which could have down-the-road benefits without additional cost.

Projected Real Savings During the Ownership Cycle

Determining whether a PZEV will make economic sense for you is an empty exercise. If you live in a state with PZEV regulations, the small car you buy will meet PZEV requirements. If you live in a state that lacks those requirements, you will get a vehicle that lacks the PZEV technology. Either way, your purchase price and overall ownership cost will be virtually identical. A PZEV does offer environmental benefits, so you have to weigh how much you value those benefits as part of the equation.

Figuring the cost-savings for buying a displacement on demand vehicle is a no-brainer for another reason. Obtaining the technology doesn't cost markedly more than buying a vehicle without it. It will get better real-world economy, so there is virtually no downside except for the niggling fear that the technology might be failure-prone. And so far, with millions of the vehicles already on the road, there is no indication of that. Another positive is the E85 capability some AFM and MDS engines offer. This could present a cost-savings opportunity depending on E85 and gasoline prices in your area. Beyond the literal cost-savings, you should also figure in the benefits of limiting our reliance on foreign fuel (at least by a small increment).

Figuring Your Ownership Cycle

To figure the cost benefits of a displacement on demand-equipped vehicle, let's put in place the vehicle ownership cost parameters we outlined in Chapter 4. To repeat, first determine how much you are paying for the vehicle and how much you expect it to be worth when you are ready to sell it. Second, determine how many miles a year you will drive. Third, estimate how much gasoline will cost during your ownership period.

Are There Real Savings?

To make the mathematics relatively simple, let's assume that the resale value of the displacement on demand vehicle and the equivalent gasoline vehicle will be the same at the end of the five-year ownership period, a reasonable expectation unless displacement on demand engines develop a bad reputation. Let's further assume that you will drive either vehicle 12,000 miles a year or 60,000 miles after 5 years. Finally, let's assume $3-a-gallon gasoline for the 5-year period. The EPA mileage for the displacement on demand vehicle is 20 miles per gallon while the equivalent gasoline vehicle gets 18 mpg combined.

That makes the cost analysis relatively easy to figure. Based on our assumptions, in a displacement on demand vehicle you will burn 3,000 gallons of gasoline to travel 60,000 miles, and at $3 a gallon that will cost you $9,000. Or in the conventionally powered vehicle, you will burn 3,333 gallons, costing you $9,999 to rack up the same number of miles.

Because we can further assume the purchase costs of the two vehicles were equal, the displacement on demand vehicle will save you $999 versus a gasoline vehicle without the fuel-saving technology. If you assume $4-a-gallon gasoline, the displacement on demand vehicle will burn up $12,000 in fuel in a typical 5-year ownership period, while the conventionally powered vehicle will use $13,332 in fuel. The displacement on demand vehicle would thus help you hold onto $1,332 that would otherwise go to fuel costs.

Who Benefits?

With PZEVs the costs are a wash, so the beneficiaries of the technology are all of us who breathe air. The vehicles are cleaner and they turn in identical fuel economy. Win-win.

With displacement on demand technology everybody wins as well, because the vehicles cost no more to purchase and they get better mileage. How much you save, though, depends both on how much you drive and what kind of driving you do. Those who do a great deal of stop-and-go freeway or around-town driving will benefit less than those who do a great deal of highway driving. That's because the displacement on demand system will spend more driving time in partial-cylinder mode rather than full-cylinder mode on long, straight stretches of highway.

Displacement on demand vehicles are just marginally better than conventional engines in exhaust emission performance, but, because they burn less fuel, they do help somewhat in the war against CO_2 emissions. And they do help mitigate our reliance on foreign sources of crude oil. As we noted, because they are already on the road in reasonably large numbers, they will save millions of gallons of gasoline each year.

Who won't benefit from a displacement on demand vehicle? If a substantial portion of your driving is done in town, you won't get much benefit from the new technology. On the other hand, because obtaining the technology is virtually cost-free, any improvement you do get will be a bonus.

Currently Available Models

As we noted, PZEV capability is currently offered on some 30 different models from a variety of domestic, European, and Asian manufacturers. Most of the vehicles are small cars that get relatively good fuel mileage. Displacement on demand technology is now offered on an increasing variety of models from Chrysler Group and General Motors. Generally, vehicles in this category are large sedans, full-size sport utility vehicles, or full-size pickup trucks. Models with these capabilities have essentially the same attributes and performance as similar conventional gasoline-only vehicles. See Appendix D for more details.

The Least You Need to Know

- The gasoline engine, though much maligned, is constantly evolving for the better in terms of both fuel economy and emissions.

- PZEVs offer significantly lower exhaust emissions than contemporary conventional vehicles of the same size and weight.

- Displacement on demand vehicles, usually large sedans and trucks, offer 5 to 10 percent better fuel economy than conventional vehicles and generally cost no more.

- Although PZEVs offer no real cost savings, they do benefit us by delivering cleaner exhaust.

- Displacement on demand vehicles offer 5 to 10 percent fuel and cost savings, but have relatively little effect on air quality.

Chapter 9

Electric Cars

In This Chapter

- ◆ Putting electric tech in perspective
- ◆ Learning the current state of electric vehicles
- ◆ Living life in the electric lane
- ◆ Matching the electric buzz with savings

No vehicle type in the pantheon of vehicles generates the emotional charge that electric cars do. Proponents of the technology are not just admirers of the electric vehicle's many benefits, a substantial portion of them also seem to have a strong emotional investment in the concept. Simply put, they *love* their electric cars, and they believe electric cars are the right way—perhaps *the only way*—for personal transportation to go.

Interestingly, the same phenomenon was in motion a little more than 100 years ago. While the Duryea brothers, Henry Ford, and Ransom E. Olds tinkered with cars powered by internal combustion engines, other visionaries believed the goal of efficient personal transport could be achieved more simply by using electricity. In fact both Ford and Olds toyed with electrics even as they moved forward in fits and starts with their efforts to perfect the intricacies of employing gasoline engines in vehicles small and practical enough to be viable consumer products.

It is not hard to see why so many gravitated toward electric propulsion. Compared to harnessing the power from an internal combustion engine, designing an effective electric-powered car was a piece of cake. The first electric vehicle was constructed in the 1830s following the development of electric storage batteries, the required source of portable power. The initial failing with the storage batteries used in that contraption was that they were nonrechargeable. This meant that after they ran out of power—where they actually exhausted the material that, when combined, produced a flow of electric current—the batteries had to be replaced just as the batteries in your flashlight. That major issue was addressed by Gaston Plante. In 1859, he introduced the first rechargeable lead-acid battery.

Electricity Is a Logical Choice

In 1889, Thomas Edison—Mr. Electricity himself—built an electric car using nickel-alkaline batteries as the power storage medium. Meanwhile, other tinkers in the United States and in Europe saw the simple wisdom of wiring lead-acid batteries through a simple controller to an electric motor. The motor drove one or more wheels of the resulting "car." The arrangement was simple and reliable. Unlike a gasoline car, the electric car didn't require "starting." When you wanted to go, you simply directed electric current from the battery or batteries to the electric motor. When you wanted it to go faster, you simply directed more current to the motor. Add some brakes to get it to stop and a steering system so you could direct it, and you had yourself a reasonable, practical, personal conveyance system.

In contrast the internal combustion engine (ICE) was, and continues to be, much more needy and temperamental. Unlike an electric motor, the typical ICE requires a system of gears to channel its torque to the drive wheels; it requires a clutch to launch from a stop without stalling; it requires a throttle mechanism to regulate the speed of the engine; and, of course, it requires a special mechanism simply to start the engine in the first place. Of course, you have to steer it and stop it, too. So you can see the complications, and that's just looking at the engineering problem in the simplest terms.

With this as background you can see why in 1900 the majority of the cars on the road were electric cars, and by a ratio that some experts estimate was 10 to 1. Vehicle makers who would eventually make a name for themselves as build-ers of gasoline-powered cars, Oldsmobile and Studebaker among them, assembled elec-tric cars. Other manufacturers, including Waverly, Rauch & Lang; Detroit Electric; Baker; and Columbia and Pope, built electric cars, delivery vehicles, ambulances, and trucks. Because they were silent, electrics were especially appropriate as hearses.

 Boosters

Talk about taking that one last ride .... In 1901, President William McKinley was wheeled away from the assassination attempt that eventually took his life in an electric ambu-lance.

A Hurdle Electrics Couldn't Jump

Then, as now, the major stumbling block for electric cars revolved around a question of range. Batteries can only store a finite amount of power, and when that power is exhausted they must be recharged before they can resume supplying electricity to the motor or other application. Even the best of modern batteries can store only a small percentage of the energy of a gallon of gasoline in the same space. In 1910, battery and recharging technology had not advanced to today's level. As drivers of those newfangled automobiles began to venture farther and farther from home, a driving range of 40 or 50 miles before a recharge just didn't cut it. Gasoline cars, for all their failings, could go much farther on a tank of gas. In addition, when they ran out of gas, the driver could refuel and get going again. In contrast, recharging a battery bank took hours.

The final death knell for the first wave of electric vehicles came in 1912 with Charles Kettering's development of the self-starter. Ironically, Kettering used an electric motor wired to a storage battery to power his starter. It made gasoline cars infinitely more practical because it removed the onerous and often dangerous task of starting the engine by jerking a crank. Up until the invention of the self-starter, many men and women had chosen electric cars because they did not want to fool with crank-starting their vehicle. After its introduction, gasoline car sales began to boom and electrics fell by the wayside.

What Are Modern Electric Vehicles?

After their first meteoric rise and fall, electric cars essentially disappeared for decades. It wasn't until the late 1960s that they saw renewed interest. That interest was prompted by changes the gasoline-powered car had wrought on our skies in the intervening 50 years. With smog and air pollution a hot topic—and the prospect of inexpensive nuclear-generated electricity on the near horizon—engineers around the globe began taking another look at electric cars.

But the problem of limited range remained the paramount stumbling block, and no one had the solution although several approaches, including hybrid gasoline-electric combinations, were tried on an experimental basis. Finally it took legislation and looming regulations from the powerful California Air Resources Board (CARB) to get auto manufacturers off the dime on the development of a modern electric car.

In its continuing battle to fight air pollution, in 1990, CARB instituted the historic Zero Emission Vehicle (ZEV) mandate. It dictated that just 8 years later, in 1998, 2 percent of the vehicles sold in the state of California had to emit virtually no pollutants at all. That figure was also slated to grow to 10 percent by 2003.

This long-rumored edict struck fear in the hearts of auto manufacturers. To sell vehicles in the large and lucrative California market, a market bigger than that of Canada, they would be forced to find ways to engineer, develop, and sell ZEVs in numbers that would represent at least 2 percent of their total vehicle volume. To many of them, that was more than a tall order, it was virtually impossible to do on their own. Smaller manufacturers looked to bigger manufacturers such as General Motors, Ford, Honda, and Toyota, hoping the big fish would design and engineer ZEVs and then allow them to buy some to sell on their own. But the large manufacturers were looking at their own problems, namely putting together ZEVs that consumers might actually want to buy. Because CARB was not about to waver on the zero-emissions requirement, the only feasible way to get there was to build electric cars.

So they moved their fledgling electric vehicle (EV) efforts forward and developed vehicles they hoped California consumers would accept. General Motors decided to get ahead of the game with its Impact, which was quickly renamed the GM EV1 and introduced to the public with a clever marketing campaign. Ford, Honda, and Toyota all adopted lower profiles, but all would eventually introduce electric vehicles to the California market in anticipation of the 1998 deadline. Ford's choice was, counter-intuitively, a compact pickup truck; Toyota decided its RAV4 compact sport utility vehicle would make a good EV; and Honda settled on the completely nondescript EV Plus.

What happened next is open to interpretation, depending on your political and environmental persuasion. Some say the electric cars, including the highly visible EV1, were stupendous successes. Others say they were dismal failures and proved that it was impossible to interest even 2 percent of the buying public in purchasing or leasing a ZEV, which was, of course, an EV. Some owners/lessees absolutely loved their electric cars and trucks, but others discovered what owners of Baker and Waverly electrics had discovered in 1910, that their limited range of maybe 70 or 80 miles on a charge made them impractical for many uses. Conspiracy theorists believe that the manufacturers intentionally put poorly performing vehicles into the market in an attempt to kill the electric car.

Whether you buy that notion or not, the effect of the limited sale of EVs and their experiences in the real-world persuaded CARB to back off from its mandates. They decided to attack air pollution in other, less direct ways. With the monkey off their backs after the requirement to sell 10 percent ZEVs by 2003 was dropped, the auto manufacturers quickly bailed out of the electric vehicle business altogether. Most famously, GM refused to renew the leases on all the EV1s that were on the streets, forcing drivers to return them. The cars were eventually crushed. A few electric Ford Rangers and Toyota RAV4s are still out there, but they are orphans of the storm.

So if you are looking to buy a new electric vehicle from a major auto manufacturer, something you could have done earlier in the decade, you are out of luck. A few smaller companies do offer electric vehicles, but they are far from mainstream. They range from rudimentary Neighborhood Electric Vehicles (NEVs) that offer maximum speeds of 30 mph to exotic, hand-built specialty sports cars with shockingly impressive performance and prodigious price tags.

How Do Electric Vehicles Work?

Fascinatingly, the real answer to this question is that nobody seems to know. Even the world's most brilliant scientists admit that they don't know how electricity works or why it works; they simply know it does work. That philosophical concept aside, an electric vehicle uses batteries to power an electric motor that, in turn, propels the vehicle. Vehicles that have these characteristics are alternatively called *pure electric vehicles.*

> **? Definitions**
>
> A **pure electric vehicle** uses on-board sources of electricity stored in a battery or battery bank as power, and it must be plugged into a source of electricity to recharge its batteries. It is otherwise known as a battery electric vehicle or BEV.

Electric cars produce no tailpipe emissions and the miniscule amounts of "evaporative emissions" they produce come from the evaporation of their lubricants. The vehicle's batteries must be recharged from the "electrical grid," which in practice means a power hook-up at your home and/or office. Many electric vehicles also use "regenerative braking," a procedure that generates electricity when the car is slowing down or coasting.

Electric drive systems are virtually nonpolluting and extremely energy efficient. Although only about 20 percent of the chemical energy in gasoline is converted into useful work at the wheels of an internal combustion vehicle, some 75 percent or more of the energy from a battery reaches the wheels of an EV. This helps make up for the fact that current battery technology does not allow the storage of nearly as much energy as is contained in the gas tank of a conventional car.

A key advantage of an electric motor is its ability to provide power and torque at almost any engine speed. In contrast, internal combustion engines produce their peak horsepower and torque in relatively narrow ranges of engine speed, hence an elaborate system of gears (in common parlance, a "transmission") is required to keep the engine operating in its sweet spot while the car travels at varying velocities. Electric motors provide nearly peak power even at very low revolutions per minute (rpm), and this gives electric vehicles strong acceleration performance from a stop.

Just as it was in 1910, it is the quality of the batteries that determine the cost, performance, and essential viability of EVs. The EVs from the major manufacturers that came to market and then left the market as the millennium turned used lead-acid batteries, the same type of battery that electric cars used at the turn of the previous century. By the way, that same type of battery powers the starter motor and radio in your current car. Now there are several new types of automotive batteries available and under development, including advanced lead-acid batteries, nickel-metal hydride, lithium-polymer, and lithium-ion. Still, even the best of these new batteries can hold only a tiny faction of the energy "stored" in a gallon of gasoline in the same space. What this means is that driving range is still a major issue.

This could be addressed at least to some extent by the ability to quickly recharge the on-board batteries. However, even in the best of today's systems, recharging still takes a considerable amount of time, much longer than filling up your car's gas tank. On the positive side, relatively simple home recharging systems are available. They can serve as a convenient way to fill batteries with power every night without ever having to go to a filling station. But while that can be a boon, recharging sites away from home are still scarce.

The Pluses and Minuses of Battery-Powered Electric Vehicles

Electric vehicles, especially pure electric BEVs, are the darlings of hardcore environmentalists because they don't pollute. Period. There are no "tailpipe emissions" at all. How could there be? There are no tailpipes. And the evaporative emissions are so small, they're not even worth noting. Greenhouse gas emissions? Forget it. BEVs are clean, clean, clean.

That being said, the electricity that goes through the grid and into the storage batteries of each electric car has to come from somewhere.

This has led to very complicated analyses of the overall environmental impact of the process of electrical generation, transmission, and delivery versus other energy sources. For gasoline, an analogous trail takes you from oil well, through pipeline, to refinery, to gas station, to the tank of your car and, finally, out the exhaust system. Although we won't bore you with the details of this "well-to-wheels" analysis, suffice it to say that electric vehicles come out way ahead on the nonpolluting scale.

In the United States, the largest portion of our electricity is generated by coal-fired generating plants. That might sound "dirty" but the best of today's coal generating stations emit minimal amounts of pollution. Generation plants that use natural gas or gas produced from coal are even cleaner overall, and wind, water, and geothermal sources of electricity are virtually pollution-free. So is nuclear power, for that matter, but most environmentalists don't want to go there.

> **Boosters**
>
> Coal is not only the fuel that fostered the Industrial Revolution, but it could also be the fuel that fosters our Post-Industrial Age, because estimates indicate there are enough coal reserves to last 300 years.

In addition to the good news on the environmental front, EVs offer good news in the quest to limit our use of foreign oil. More than 95 percent of the electricity used to charge EVs originates from domestic resources. For example, the United States possesses huge amounts of coal and bountiful supplies of natural gas. Solar power is another largely untapped source that could be employed in each household and workplace to charge electric vehicles.

Because electric motors are so efficient, EVs also have a positive story to tell on the operating costs front. Electricity rates vary widely across the country, but no matter what the cost of a kilowatt hour in your locale, driving an EV will almost certainly be less expensive than driving a conventional gasoline-powered car. After you own it, that is.

Which brings us to the primary (and some would say monumental) downside of electric vehicles—they can be very expensive. Why? Batteries, that's why. To store the amount of energy required to give them acceptable range, electric vehicles need substantial battery capacity, and those batteries are expensive. Many of them use relatively expensive base materials, and those materials then have to be combined and crafted into functioning electricity storage modules. Although electric motors and the controllers that operate them are pretty cheap in the overall scheme of things and very efficient to boot, the batteries needed to power them are worlds more expensive than installing an empty container designed to be filled with gasoline or diesel.

In addition, there is the need for a recharging system. Obviously a conventional gasoline car doesn't need to be "recharged"; in essence, it is recharged every time you fill its tank with gas. In contrast, batteries need to be recharged frequently, and you, as the owner of the EV, are required to have the equipment to do that. Publicly available recharging stations are few and far between. The equipment is not prohibitively expensive (and often it is built into the EV itself), but it adds further expense.

The big question is, could the price of batteries and charging equipment go down significantly if manufacturers were to scale up for big-time electric vehicle production? The answer to that is more complicated than a simple yes or no. Some portions of the process would undoubtedly benefit from economies of scale, but other portions, such as battery production that requires the use of scarce natural resources (sound familiar?), would realize only partial benefits. Batteries still could be very expensive.

Potholes

There are very few publicly accessible places to recharge your electric car. Even if there were thousands more, the long recharge required to bring batteries back to full power limits their usefulness.

Boosters

If you commute less than 80 miles roundtrip, an electric car can be a great choice. You can recharge it every night at home; it will operate for pennies a mile; and in many jurisdictions you can use the high occupancy vehicle (carpool) lane even if you're alone in the car.

Driving an Electric Vehicle Day-to-Day

Well-designed EVs can travel at the same speeds as conventional vehicles and can offer the same safety and convenience capabilities as conventional gasoline-powered vehicles. Even though many expect EVs to be slow and sluggardly to drive, EVs generally offer better acceleration than you would expect because of the high-torque characteristics of electric motors at low speeds. One sports-oriented electric car that is now on the market can accelerate from 0 to 60 mph in the same time as a Ferrari.

Many EVs, such as the famous and now out-of-production EV1, are small. That's largely because vehicle weight is an enemy of vehicle range. The more weight the electric motor has to propel, the more electricity it will require. Because of this, EV engineers are very particular about weight. For the same reason, they pay a great deal of attention to other items that draw electrical power, things such as heating and air conditioning and even sound systems. Unlike gasoline cars that have virtually unlimited sources of electricity to fuel these functions, EVs must ration electricity or lose their range.

Range is the key factor when driving an EV, and keeping your eye on the gauge that tracks available electrical power is important. A further complication is that range varies with the number of passengers, payload, weather, and the use of heating and air conditioning and even the sound system. Although some EVs claim greater theoretical range, in practical situations EVs are limited to 50 to 130 miles before they need a recharge. For around-town hops and most commutes that's fine, but kiss cross-country trips good-bye.

> **Boosters**
>
> If you spend 15 minutes a week buying gasoline at a filling station, recharging your electric vehicle at home could save you 13 hours a year.

Safety

Like all new cars and trucks sold in the United States, EVs must meet all federal motor vehicle safety requirements. One negative factor EVs present in terms of safety is their small size and weight. In collisions the vehicle with the greater mass usually gets the best of it but, on the other hand, EVs' easy-to-maneuver size and surprisingly quick acceleration might enable them to avoid accidents other, more lumbering vehicles, might get into. Electric vehicles can be equipped with all the common safety equipment, including multiple airbags, antilock brakes, and electronic stability control.

Some might worry about driving in a vehicle filled with high-voltage electrical wires and batteries. However, the batteries are sealed and all high-voltage circuits are protected from casual contact. In addition, high-voltage wiring and circuits are marked, color-coded, and posted with warnings. Largely because there are so many gasoline-electric hybrids on the road today, most emergency response teams are trained in proper procedures for dealing with high-voltage wiring in case of accidents.

Boosters

If you wonder about the danger from electric shock when you're recharging your vehicle, don't worry. If you can plug in a toaster without electrocuting yourself, you can safely recharge an EV.

We've established electric cars are safe, but safety is only part of the issue when it comes to insurance. The overriding factor with an electric vehicle is its rarity. As a specialized product, it will most likely be more expensive to insure than a conventional vehicle.

Reliability

Simplicity usually translates to longevity and reliability, and that is the case with electric vehicles. Properly maintained it is conceivable they will run forever (or at least longer than you or I will live). Further, because they are so simple, EVs require very little maintenance. They don't have crankcases so there is no oil to change; they don't burn anything so there is no need for fuel filters, air filters, spark plugs, fuel injectors, or radiators. Keep the batteries charged and fill the windshield washer fluid reservoir when it's nearly empty, and you're there.

The only bit of special attention they insist on is keeping an eye on the state of the batteries and the charging system. Because you can't go anywhere without charged batteries, this is crucial. The batteries don't like extreme heat or cold, and they should be charged in moderate temperatures. Luckily, it is not difficult. In modern hybrids and future pure electrics, charge current is not directed to the batteries until they are at a proper temperature. This does not mean that electric cars can't be parked outdoors; though, like gasoline cars, they might function a bit better if they are routinely garaged.

Cost to Repair

We can tell you one thing. The local independent auto repair shop or dealership service center you patronize probably doesn't have a qualified electric vehicle technician. Although some EV systems, such as brakes for example, are similar to those in a conventional car, virtually everything else is different, way different. Most often this will mean premium prices when it comes time to get the vehicle repaired.

On a more positive note, as we detailed earlier, very little maintenance is needed. In addition, EVs don't feature any pieces that are prone to break. Electric motors are amazingly reliable and durable. Battery packs should be good for five to seven years of service if not more, depending on battery type. Newer nickel-metal hydride and lithium-ion batteries have lengthy life expectancies. But if and when they do fail, look out. Replacing them will be mucho-expensive, in the neighborhood of several thousand dollars.

Cost to Operate

The cost of operation of an electric vehicle recharged using your electricity at home can be amazingly low. Rates for electricity vary widely by region and even by local community. Most residential rates are tightly regulated by public utility commissions, and in many areas electricity is supplied by publicly owned municipal power providers. So it is difficult to state exactly how great the savings are versus a gasoline car. But suffice it to say, they are substantial.

Purchase Price

There is more to obtaining an electric vehicle than simply paying the price. First you must find a manufacturer offering a vehicle that really can be called a car. With GM, Toyota, Ford, Honda, and Nissan out of the EV market, the mantle of the electric car movement has been picked up by a variety of much smaller companies. Some, such as Myers Motors and Zap, offer three-wheel electric vehicles that have some car-like characteristics but are officially characterized as motorcycles. The Myers NmG (for "no more gas") retails for around $25,000. The Zap Xebra, which has a top speed of just 40 mph by the way, retails for around $10,000.

AC Propulsion is close to building an electric version of the popular Scion xB, but instead of the $15,000 or so one would pay for the gasoline version of the car at a Toyota dealer, the converted version is expected to retail for about $75,000 (and that's no misprint). Tesla Motors is hopeful of selling 700 examples of its all-electric reworking of the Lotus Elite sports car. The asking price for that two-seater with excellent performance potential and decent range is $89,000. In comparison, a gasoline-powered Elite sells for about half as much.

If all this has you gulping, there are a few ways to get less-expensive electric vehicles. One is to convert a car or truck to electric power. There is more on that in the next chapter. Perhaps the best way is to track down a used EV that escaped the crusher. For instance, as this is being written, a 1998 Ford Ranger EV is up for bid at eBay Motors, and it will likely be purchased for less than $10,000. Other used EVs are for sale by owners and dealers as well, but the quantities are very limited and the quality and reliability vary significantly.

Projected Real Savings During the Ownership Cycle

As you might guess from the above discussion, the projected "savings" during the ownership cycle of an electric vehicle versus a gasoline-powered vehicle hinge in large measure on how much you pay for the electric vehicle. As we have seen, the premium for a new electric versus its gasoline-only equivalent is mind-boggling, often 100 percent or more. It would be hard to imagine any scenario in which a new EV would provide a cost benefit when compared with an equivalent gasoline vehicle. On the other hand, if you can live with an EV's peculiarities, especially when it comes to range, an electric car or truck might offer cost benefits when purchased used.

Figuring Your Ownership Cycle

For the sake of argument, let's run an EV comparison versus a gasoline car using the vehicle ownership cost parameters we outlined in Chapter 4. To repeat, first determine how much you are paying for the vehicle and how much you expect it to be worth when you are ready to sell it. Second, determine how many miles a year you will drive. Third, estimate how much your electricity and gasoline will cost during your ownership period.

Are There Real Savings?

As we noted, electricity costs vary considerably depending on where you live in the United States. Because of that we believe it is most instructive to use the Department of Energy's electricity-gasoline equivalency values in our comparison.

To make our example relatively simple, let's assume the resale value of the electric and the gasoline car will be the same at the end of the five-year ownership period. Let's further assume that you will drive either car 12,000 miles a year or 60,000 miles after 5 years. Finally, let's assume $2.31-a-gallon gasoline for the 5-year period and a $2.71-a-gallon electricity price (both taken from DOE data). The EPA mileage for the gasoline vehicle in our comparison is 26 mpg, and the DOE-calculated miles-per-gallon equivalency of the electric vehicle is a staggering 104 mpg.

That makes the cost-benefit analysis decently simple. Based on our assumptions, you will burn 2,308 gallons of gasoline to travel your 60,000 miles, and at $2.31-a-gallon that will cost you $5,331. In stark contrast, the EV will use the electric equivalent of 577 gallons of $2.71-a-gallon gasoline (again using the DOE conversion). This means in fuel cost, you would pay $1,564 to go the same distance. That gives a startling $3,767 advantage to the EV.

Now, as you can see, the projected benefit or loss depends on purchase price. Any new EV (with the possible exception of the Myers NmG) has no hope of providing a cost benefit larger than the equivalent gasoline car. We're not even considering the Zap Xebra at all because with a top speed of just 40 mph, it realistically can't be compared to a real car. The bottom-line on EVs: the price premium is far too steep to be overcome by the potential cost savings, even if they are eye-popping.

Federal, state, and local tax credits can help even the score somewhat. Credits as high as $5,000 do exist, but they are far too complex to outline here. A good summary of the available credits is available at www. eere.energy.gov/afdc/laws/incen_laws.html. Still, even with tax credits, it is hard to make an economic case for electric cars.

Who Benefits?

When trying to determine if you would benefit from owning an EV, we strongly recommend you take a long, hard look at how much you drive, where you drive, how long you drive, and your tolerance for hassle. Frankly, these days it takes a rugged individualist to get comfortable with an electric vehicle. In doing this self-analysis, you should also assess what value you put in driving a cleaner, greener vehicle and one that contributes to limiting our country's reliance on foreign oil, because by our measure that is an electric vehicle's most positive attribute.

Because electric vehicles aren't well-suited for long-distance driving, an individual with a short commute or who makes many in-city starts and stops is a prime candidate for owning an EV. A person in either of those circumstances can recharge the vehicle's batteries at home every night, so the lack of recharging stations and the length of time needed to recharge are moot. Qualifying to drive alone in the carpool lane is another potential benefit to urban dwellers.

If you need to drive cross country or if your everyday driving takes you more than 80 miles or so, an EV won't do the job for you. And if you want to buy a new EV and have it serviced locally, you probably can forget about that as well. These days living with an EV requires a bit of stubbornness and more than a little perseverance—qualities we respect but realize not everyone possesses.

Guide to Currently Available Models

A guide to the currently available vehicles is short, and it is important to note that none of the major manufacturers build or warrant any of the currently built models.

Myers NmG

Running on three wheels, this impish single-seater is technically a motorcycle.

Zap Xebra

Another three-wheeler, the Xebra, which can be had with a zebra-stripe paint job, is inexpensive but has a top speed of just 40 mph.

Tesla Roadster

Tesla took a two-seat Lotus Elite sports coupe, and stuffed it with batteries. It offers both excellent acceleration and a better-than-expected range of some 200 miles on a charge. But it's not cheap.

AC Propulsion xB Conversion

Another modification of a conventional passenger car, the AC Propulsion version of the Scion xB offers acceptable performance and range, but at a price more than three times that of the car on which it is based.

The Least You Need to Know

◆ Electric vehicles are clean, clean, clean—no tailpipe emissions at all, miniscule evaporative emissions, and no emissions of greenhouse gases.

◆ Vehicle range is an EV's big failing. Most are lucky to travel 100 miles on a charge. Their batteries must then be recharged before further travel is possible.

◆ You will pay far more for an electric vehicle than for an equivalent gasoline vehicle. Electric vehicle mechanics are also hard to find so service will be expensive.

◆ After they have been purchased, electric vehicles can run for just pennies a mile, far less per-mile than a gasoline car.

Chapter 10

What About My Car?

In This Chapter

- ◆ Switching your car's identity
- ◆ Building hybrids at home
- ◆ Flexing your power
- ◆ Knowing if your car is a gas
- ◆ Finding that grease is the word

Certainly buying a new hybrid or alt-fuel vehicle is an appealing way to go about joining the fray against environmental pollution and the nation's dependence on overseas energy sources. Is it a way of saving money in the face of rising fuel shortages? For most of us, probably not. Doing the middle school mathematics on the issue, you will likely find that keeping your current car—if it is in reasonable operating condition—will save you money versus purchasing something new. Of course, unless you have an alt-fuel car already, keeping your current vehicle will do nothing to battle against exhaust emissions, the use of fossil fuel, or our thirst for foreign petroleum.

What this might conjure up in your mind is the thought of converting your present vehicle to some alternative propulsion method, anything from changing it into a hybrid to switching its fuel from gasoline to salad dressing. Given the high and volatile price of gasoline recently, it is not hard to see the hopeful appeal of such a swap. Gas is costly so switching away from gas will probably not be as costly, the thinking goes. And the fact is you can alter your vehicle to run on alternative fuels, and you can even turn it into a hybrid of sorts, but the simple question to be asked is "How much are you willing to spend to save money?" Appealing as the prospect of limiting or eliminating your use of gasoline may be, you will find the cost of making a switch to be serious (sometimes prohibitive) and the process often daunting.

Your chances of success in this area depend on two things. First, which conversion you want to undertake, because some are certainly more easily accomplished than others. Second, your manual dexterity, skill with tools, and ability to follow sometimes complex instructions.

And if you want to throw a third thing in there, success may also depend on the amount of money you are willing to devote to the conversion process. Similar to a home remodeling project, it will almost undoubtedly cost more than you might at first expect.

Converting to Hybrid Power?

In 1979, in the midst of a severe "fuel crisis," Dave Arthurs of Springdale, Arkansas, spent $1,500 converting his conventionally powered Opel GT into a hybrid vehicle. His revamped Opel reportedly got 75 miles per gallon, which is jaw-dropping efficiency even when compared to today's Toyota Prius. Arthurs' creation combined a substantial 400-amp electric motor with a collection of six-volt batteries for motive power, while a six-horsepower lawnmower-type engine was used to keep the battery bank in a reasonable state of charge.

Potholes

Though 60,000 people requested hybrid vehicle plans from *Mother Earth News*, considerably fewer than 60,000 of those hybrids were ever built—which shows you the pitfalls of trying to convert a car from one technology to another.

After learning about Arthurs' successful foray into the then utterly arcane world of hybrid vehicles, the magazine *Mother Earth News* got in the act and built a similar vehicle using Arthurs' basic plans. Their hybrid reportedly got more than 80 miles per gallon, and it so excited readers in that time of overheated gasoline prices and iffy supply that 60,000 people requested copies of the plans.

The lesson from the *Mother Earth News* experience—great interest but little follow-through—is two-fold. First, it is possible for even a back-yard mechanic to build a hybrid vehicle. Second, you have to wonder if it is worth the effort given the quality of the driving experience of the vehicle that will result from your hard work. Building any operating car—hybrid or not—is a difficult task. Building a hybrid that functions much like a "conventional" car is especially difficult.

Before you embark on such a project I suggest you ask yourself what you would like the results to be. Do you want a vehicle that will function in much the same manner as a conventional gasoline car in areas such as speed, range, comfort, handling, and overall drivability? Or are you willing to make some tradeoffs in these areas?

I'm not stacking the deck here one way or another. There are no definitive right and wrong answers to these questions. Some of us want our alt-fuel vehicles to perform much as a conventional vehicle, while others are content to make trade-offs, feeling it is worth the sacrifice to save fuel and the environment. You have to applaud those who are willing to make the sacrifices, too.

Suffice it to say that if you want your hybrid car to mimic your gasoline car in most facets of operation and improve on your current car in fuel economy and exhaust emissions, you are well-advised to buy a hybrid built by a major manufacturer, either new or used. Car makers have the resources and the techniques to develop and test their vehicles to meet a wide variety of standards and expectations. You simply don't have the technical knowledge or the developmental time and resources to do this.

The technology that enables the current crop of hybrids marketed by auto manufacturers to have gained such great acceptance in the market is not engine technology but instead computer technology. It is the highly sophisticated computer controls that allow the shifting of power sources to occur so seamlessly. Of major importance is the ability to utilize a combined gasoline engine and electric motor driving mode.

The complexity of that task is enormous, significantly more complex than hooking up a go-kart engine to run a generator that charges some golf cart batteries, which in turn powers an electric motor that drives the vehicle. Yes, such a vehicle is a hybrid, but to most of us it is unacceptable for everyday use.

Converting Hybrids to Hybrids

Although converting a conventional car to an acceptable hybrid is a very daunting task, converting a hybrid to a more efficient vehicle is not nearly as challenging. Such a conversion can be accomplished by giving the hybrid car plug-in capability, or it can be accomplished by altering the computer programs that run the conventional hybrid (he said oxymoronically).

Giving a hybrid such as a Prius plug-in capability can be achieved by installing additional battery capacity and controlling that added capability with hardware and software tweaks. The goal of the conversion is to enable the hybrid to travel much more frequently and for a longer duration in electric-only mode. Mymotion and EDrive are two companies that specialize in this type of conversion. One source of information on this is www.edrivesystems.com.

Changing Hybrid Software

Executing a hybrid conversion is somewhat tricky but not beyond the bounds of reason; making a change in the hybrid hardware and software that will allow the vehicle to perform better is an even trickier task. Such an alteration has been made on a few examples of the Honda Insight, the first modern hybrid to go on sale in America. However, the change was not to make the controlling software more sophisticated, as you might guess. Instead, the alteration offered the driver more control of the battery charge-discharge process. Thus a very skilled driver-operator could get additional range and fuel economy by adapting the vehicle operation and its battery charging to subtle nuances that could escape the on-board computer system's capabilities.

Although this operation reportedly offered positive results in range and mileage in the hands of skilled hybrid drivers, it is unlikely the average driver would want to go to this extreme in monitoring and controlling his or her vehicle. Even more importantly, newer, more sophisticated hybrid systems out-perform a human-aided system of charge activation. The systems have essentially gotten smarter than we are.

Converting to Flex Fuel?

As I outlined in Chapter 5, there are millions of vehicles on the road today that have Flex Fuel capability. The fact is that most of those are operating every day on gasoline rather than E85, so they are doing nothing to improve our air quality or fight consumption of overseas oil. Before embarking on a conversion of your current vehicle to E85 capability, you might be better advised to sell your current vehicle and buy a new or used Flex Fuel vehicle. Because those vehicles command virtually no premium versus conventional new or used cars, you can go that route with virtually no penalty. You get all the advantages of a carmaker engineered and built system, and if you buy new, it will be accompanied by a lengthy factory warranty against defects.

That being said, if you are adamant about converting your current vehicle into being E85-capable, there are companies that can help with the conversion. FlexTek is a Flex Fuel conversion technology that utilizes its own standalone computer processor to enable the vehicle's fuel system to burn ethanol, gasoline, or any blend of the two fuels, according to its manufacturer. It essentially adds a second computer controller to sense the characteristics of the fuel being burned and to alter engine settings to accommodate that. According to the manufacturer, the vehicle's original computer is not bypassed. The vehicle continues to be controlled by the original sensors and engine control unit (ECU) but in such a way as to allow efficient burning of alcohol blends.

The FlexTek system, which costs between $500 and $1,000 depending on engine type, plugs into the vehicle's existing wiring harness without cutting or splicing. And its maker says it is easily removed leaving your car completely unaltered.

Well, yes and no, because what is unclear but potentially troubling is the effect running E85 will have on engine and fuel system parts. Because ethanol is more corrosive than gasoline, auto manufacturers switch out fuel system and valvetrain components to more corrosion-resistant materials when they convert their conventional gasoline engines to Flex Fuel use. Instead of going to this time-consuming and costly step,

FlexTek "highly recommends" that users of its conversion system "treat" their engines with the included E85 Engine Preparation Kit before running on alcohol. The kit is a combination of engine treatment chemicals that is said to help clean the fuel system and protect the engine from corrosion.

The engine treatment is a proprietary formula designed to protect against acids produced by E85 fuel. These chemicals must be added to clean crankcase oil, and the vehicle should then be run for at least 2,000 miles on gasoline before beginning to use E85, according to FlexTek. Though this formula could well work, I am skeptical that it can properly protect against corrosion and potential fuel system failure.

Another issue with the conversion is that, because it alters the operation of the ECU, a key component of a modern engine's fuel economy and pollution control system, it could be a violation of the federal Clean Air Act. FlexTek deals with that possibility this way: "The EPA has actually condoned converting vehicles, saying '... consumers who want existing vehicles to accommodate ethanol-blended gasoline beyond E10 might have to modify engines ...' They [EPA] never suggest that such modification may be subject to EPA certification. Also, according to the EPA, our modification does not violate the anti-tampering law as long as we have a reasonable basis for knowing that emissions are not adversely affected. We do have a reasonable basis for knowing that emissions are not adversely affected."

Based on that information, you can make up your own mind on the advisability of a conversion of your vehicle to Flex Fuel. More recent vehicles, which are built to function without undue corrosion when running on the commonly used E10 gasoline-ethanol mix used in many parts of the country, might fare just fine with the conversion even without changing out hard parts to more corrosion-resistant materials. The emphasis here is on the term "might." And the Environmental Protection Agency (EPA) certification issue is certainly an issue of concern.

> **Potholes**
>
> Before you embark on a conversion you should think about what is going to happen when you want to sell the vehicle. A major alteration such as a conversion can devastate its potential resale value even if the conversion is done well.

As to the cost-effectiveness of such a conversion, it is dependent on a number of variables. First, the conversion kit ranges in price from $500 to $1,000. Additionally, a professional installation is recommended, which could add several hundred dollars to the conversion process. With an initial investment of, say, $1,000 to $1,500, the payback period depends entirely on the relative local prices of gasoline and ethanol and how much you drive. You must also figure in the fact that fuel economy while running on E85 will be less, perhaps by as much as 20 percent, versus running on gasoline.

Although the conversion might not have cost-saving benefits in your situation, correctly installed, it will allow you to operate your vehicle on E85. That has the twin benefits of curbing the use of foreign oil and curbing the production of greenhouse gases. The potential violation of the Clean Air Act is disturbing, however.

Converting to Natural Gas?

As you well know, pork is the other white meat. And when it comes to automobiles, the two related gas fuels, propane and natural gas, represent the other alternative power source. Even though a great deal of general press ink has gone to gasoline-electric hybrids, propane and compressed natural gas vehicles have remained under the radar, as outlined in Chapter 6. They have excellent potential as abundant, clean-burning sources of energy.

While the auto manufacturers have concentrated on building vehicles that use compressed natural gas (CNG) while eschewing propane, the conversion side is a different story. In the conversion business, propane gets big play and natural gas is more of an adjunct.

Propane, also known as liquefied petroleum gas (LPG), has been used in vehicles since the 1920s but, as noted, no cars or light

> **Definitions**
>
> **Propane** is a gas produced during petroleum and natural gas processing. Among its desirable features is the fact that it can be relatively easily compressed to form a liquid that can be stored in transportable containers. Another feature, unlike natural gas, is that it's heavier than air so it is somewhat safer.

trucks that use propane are currently available from auto manufacturers in the United States. Despite this there are more than 200,000 propane vehicles in the United States and about 9 million worldwide. They're not all cars and light trucks, though. These numbers also include medium- and heavy-duty vehicles such as shuttles, trolleys, delivery trucks, and school buses, plus specialty vehicles such as forklifts and loaders. Propane vehicles can be equipped with dedicated fueling systems designed to use only propane or bi-fuel systems that enable fueling with either propane or gasoline.

Despite the recent push on ethanol-based E85, propane remains the easiest to purchase of the liquid and gaseous alternative fuels. All states have publicly accessible fueling stations, and there are about 3,000 across the United States. Despite some safety fears that may arise because propane is a gas, the Department of Energy (DOE) says it is safe for refueling and has a very narrow flammability range.

On the clean air front, propane vehicles produce 60 percent fewer ozone-forming emissions (CO_2 and NOX) than vehicles powered by gasoline. In addition, tests on light-duty, bi-fuel vehicles have demonstrated a 98 percent reduction in the emissions of toxics, including benzene, 1.3-butadiene, formaldehyde, and acetaldehyde, when the vehicles were running on propane rather than gasoline.

Professionally installed light-duty truck conversion to propane costs about $2,500, but the prices of conversions can vary widely. Though some fleets have found that engine service life is longer with propane and maintenance service intervals for things such as oil changes can be extended, in personal use it is prudent to maintain factory maintenance intervals.

Potholes

Propane contains about 84,000 Btu per gallon (a measure of energy content) and regular gasoline averages 114,000 Btu per gallon. That means it takes more propane than gasoline to drive the same distance.

So converting to propane won't save you money on the maintenance side, and it is doubtful that converting to propane will save you much on the fuel cost side either. If you look at the per-gallon cost of propane versus the per-gallon cost of gasoline, propane is generally cheaper. But that is balanced by the fact that propane contains less energy per gallon. According to the DOE's most recent *Clean Cities Alternative Fuel Price Report*, gasoline and propane prices on a gallon-of-gasoline equivalency basis were almost equal.

Although the news on the cost-savings front is not great, the news on where the fuel comes from is much more positive. Propane is basically a domestic resource, and approximately 85 percent of the propane used in this country results from natural gas processing and petroleum refining here in the United States.

Several companies have entered the retrofit vehicle conversion arena. One of them, AFV Solutions, Inc., received a certificate of conformity from the EPA for its propane conversion system for the 2006 model year Ford Motor Company 4.6 liter V8 gasoline engine. The conversion system is intended to be installed on the Ford Crown Victoria, Lincoln Town Car, and Mercury Grand Marquis models, cars often used in law enforcement, taxicabs, and limousine fleets. The good news on this conversion is that the AFV Solutions' dedicated propane system has passed all federal emission and operating standards required by the EPA, registering significantly below established emission limits.

A company with the slightly misleading name of Hybrid Fuel Systems, Inc. (HFS) also has recognized the potential of natural gas and propane. It has formed a multistate network of installers trained to handle systems that convert diesel and gasoline engines to operate on natural gas and propane. To become an authorized Hybrid Fuel Systems installation and service center, installers must complete a training program at the company's facilities as well as complete the conversion of a vehicle.

One interesting conversion from HFS not yet available in the United States due to emissions issues is a dual-fuel system that converts diesel engines to a mode that replaces about 80 percent of the diesel fuel with natural gas. The system relies on an engine computer to start the engine with diesel fuel and inject more natural gas and cut back on diesel as the engine speed and load increases. Compared to full-on natural gas conversions, this approach offers lower costs because no expensive engine modifications are needed. Engine power and efficiency are not diminished, and the system can be adapted to old and new diesel engines at a low cost.

What is "low cost"? In this instance the transformation is about $3,500, which takes it out of the realm of the typical consumer conversion. In fact most of these conversions are aimed at fleet operators of passenger cars or trucks. That does not mean, though, that you can't avail yourself of this technology if you have a desire to do so. Obviously, you should seek a conversion and converter that will allow your car to keep its EPA certification.

Dual-fuel conversion for typical passenger cars and light trucks is also a possibility. By using solenoid valves to open or close the flow of propane and turn on and off the gasoline fuel injection, a highly skilled auto mechanic can install a bi-fuel gasoline-propane system. Such a system requires the use of a sophisticated aftermarket engine control unit that will alter the ignition characteristics to accommodate each fuel. Of importance in this type of conversion is a strong, high-voltage spark, which might require an aftermarket ignition system and higher-quality sparkplug wires. The potential difficulty with such a conversion is adhering to the Clean Air Act regulations. Alterations of the fuel delivery system are problematic under EPA regulations despite the fact that the modifications may well result in a vehicle that emits fewer pollutants than the EPA-certified gasoline powerplant.

Converting to Biodiesel?

Compared with the mental and mechanical gymnastics involved in converting your car or truck to propane or Flex Fuel, converting your diesel-powered car or truck to biodiesel is a breeze—just fill the tank with a biodiesel fuel. According to the DOE, the various biodiesel blends available can be used in any light- or heavy-duty diesel engine.

That being said, some auto manufacturers are a little antsy about biodiesel fuel being used in their engines, so check with your owner's manual so you don't inadvertently void your warranty. In older vehicles, high-percentage blends of biodiesel (greater than 20 percent) can adversely affect fuel hoses and pump seals. And for the use of 100 percent biodiesel, hoses and gaskets should be made of materials that are compatible to the fuel. Your vehicle manufacturer is the best source of information on this.

Biodiesel fuels are available in several "flavors" in the United States. The most common blend of biodiesel is B20 (20 percent biodiesel/ 80 percent petroleum-based diesel), which is the same kind of hedge-your-bets mix as E10 gasoline. But B100 (100 percent bio-derived diesel fuel also called "neat biodiesel") and blends of less than 20 percent biologically derived diesel are available as well.

Though it is gaining popularity, biodiesel is not widely available in the United States. Using the DOE's or your state's Alternative Fuel Station Locator could help you find locations offering the fuel near your home, but it is more likely that you'll have to drive a considerable distance to purchase biodiesel. When you get there, refueling with biodiesel is safer than refueling with gasoline or petro-based diesel fuel. The flashpoint of biodiesel is significantly higher than that of conventional diesel fuel, which makes the fuel safer in general. And "neat biodiesel" is nontoxic, biodegradable, and emits fewer carcinogens in the exhaust than conventional diesel fuel. In fact, if you want to, you can drink it, but that's not advised.

> **Boosters**
>
> GreenPlan is a carbon neutralization program that allows companies to counterattack carbon emissions from their corporate fleet vehicles through tree planting. The idea is to replace the carbon dioxide emitted by company vehicles with oxygen using trees as the conversion medium. Trees pull carbon dioxide from the air into their growth process, separating the carbon and emitting oxygen as a byproduct.

Although we jest about imbibing it, biodiesel is very nearly a food. Although there are various blends, typical biodiesel is predominantly soybean oil combined with an alcohol such as methanol and a catalyst. Because it is based on something pretty pure to begin with, you might expect it to turn in good exhaust emissions performance, and you'd be right. According to the National Biodiesel Board, which is, of course, pushing the stuff, using a B20 biodiesel fuel blend will provide a 20 percent reduction in unburned hydrocarbons, a 12 percent reduction in carbon monoxide, and a 12 percent reduction in particulates such as soot. As the percentage of bio-derived stock to petrol-derived stock goes up in the fuel, the emission performance gets commensurately better.

Okay, except for availability, it's all good. What about price? Well, not so good. So far, perhaps because of limited availability (and limited competition between retail suppliers), biodiesel fuel is more expensive than petro-diesel. In general, B20 has been tracking at $0.20- to $0.40-per-gallon more than conventional diesel, while B100 has recently been selling for about 25 percent more than conventional diesel fuel. Not only that but the energy content of B100 is 10 to 12 percent lower than conventional diesel. If you fill up with B20 you basically will not be able to tell the difference, but with B100, your fuel economy will suffer perhaps 10 percent.

Because it is derived from domestic crops such as soybeans and mustard seeds, biodiesel is both renewable (we can grow more) and a buffer against foreign oil. It can also be derived from organic garbage and discarded cooking grease.

Potholes

According to Greasecar, fast food is as bad for your car as it could be for you, because many fast food restaurants use hydrogenated oils, which, while they will work in the Greasecar system, are not optimum. The key reason is that they "gel" or firm up at lower temperatures than higher-quality oils.

Speaking of discarded cooking grease, a company calling itself, amusingly, Greasecar Vegetable Fuel Systems, offers a conversion system that allows diesel vehicles to use vegetable oil as fuel. It is not technically a biodiesel system because it is designed for use with straight, unprocessed, new or used vegetable oil, while biodiesel is adulterated vegetable oil. Many Greasecar customers obtain used fry grease from local restaurants, often for free, and use it as fuel. In fact, Greasecar even gives tips on where to find the best sources of used frying oils.

Rather than simply using biodiesel in the vehicle's fuel tank, the Greasecar system is a dual-fuel, two-tank arrangement that utilizes the existing diesel tank and filters to supply diesel fuel to the engine at start-up and shutdown. After start-up, radiator coolant is used to transfer heat from the engine to the heat exchangers in the Greasecar fuel system to heat the vegetable oil in the fuel filter, lines, and fuel tank.

This is a key part of the process, because the heat reduces the viscosity of vegetable oil to a level approximating that of diesel fuel, so it can be injected into the engine properly. Equally important, when the vehicle is being shut down for a period long enough for the fuel to cool, the vegetable oil must be purged from the fuel system and replaced with diesel for the next start-up. Otherwise a nasty clog results, and you won't go anywhere.

The Greasecar conversion kit, which costs around $900, is designed for a do-it-yourself installation. Key components are the aluminum, heated fuel tank, quick-flush switching mechanism to switch between conventional diesel and vegetable oil fuels, and a 10-micron fuel filter (to take out french fries). Though designed as a do-it-yourself project, some installations are more complicated than others, so a professional installation by a Greasecar-approved installer might be a wise choice.

Given the price of conventional diesel fuel and biodiesel these days, you can see that a quick payback is possible with the Greasecar system if you get used cooking oil free from restaurants wanting you to haul it away. But suffice it to say this method of obtaining fuel is not for everybody, nor are their enough vats of onion ring and codfish grease in the country to keep us all in veggie-fuel very long. But for those who want to give the ultimate nose-thumb to "the system," Greasecar is the way.

The Least You Need to Know

◆ Converting a vehicle to a form of hybrid power is not beyond the bounds of reason, but a homebuilt hybrid won't have the drivability and user-friendliness of a commercially built hybrid car.

◆ Switching your vehicle to Flex Fuel capability prompts questions about engine longevity because E85 is a highly corrosive fuel.

◆ Propane (LPG) is the easiest to purchase of the liquid and gaseous alternative fuels, and several converters offer EPA-approved kits to turn your car into a propane vehicle.

◆ Biodiesel fuel made from soybean oil or organic waste is reaching the mainstream, but the ultimate way to say bye-bye to the oil companies is to power your vehicle with discarded french fry grease.

Chapter 11

Which Vehicle Is Right for You?

In This Chapter

- ◆ Determining rational and irrational reasons
- ◆ Finding your needs and wants
- ◆ Sorting the possibilities
- ◆ Driving with friends in cars
- ◆ Taking a look at yourself

Because you're reading this book, you undoubtedly care about your personal finances. And I think it's probably a pretty good bet that you also care about the environment, our nation's energy future, and the use of fossil fuels. You have no doubt heard of global warming and wonder how you can, in your small way, contribute to making things better rather than worse. Frankly, it is a pleasure to do the research and write this for you, because you are the right kind of people. You care about others and about the world at large. So the big question is: how do you make the right choice of vehicle that will address all these factors and your personal needs as well?

Let's start with a simple premise that I first put forth a decade ago when I wrote *The Complete Idiot's Guide to Buying or Leasing a Car*. In that tome, which has helped thousands of car buyers find the right car for them, I said this: "It is a rare person who chooses her or his vehicle for strictly practical reasons. Oh, I don't want to say it never happens. Sure it does. Occasionally it snows in Los Angeles, too. But buying a car for sound, rational, dollars-and-sense reasons is certainly not the norm."

That was true then. It is true now. Each of us chooses our vehicle for complex reasons that say as much about us as they do about the vehicle we end up with. Many of us try to justify our vehicle purchases by giving a lot of plausible rational reasons that led us to our decisions, but most of the time I believe that the decision is made as much by the heart as by the head. And there's nothing wrong with that. We don't buy our homes or our clothes because they are "cost-effective," do we? So why should we do that with our cars?

Take Stock of Yourself

Of any group that I could be writing for, I have confidence that the readers of this book will make the right choices for themselves and for the earth. Why? Because I have the abiding belief that you are concerned about not only your own situation but also the big picture. In fact, your concern about the big picture is likely the reason you picked up this book in the first place.

So let's take a look at your needs and wants, the two basic categories of "reasons for purchase." Needs are fairly simple to address, because most of us who drive passenger cars, SUVs, minivans, and pickup trucks actually have pretty similar needs. Among them are:

- ◆ Commuting to and from work
- ◆ Shopping and running errands
- ◆ Transporting other people
- ◆ Transporting stuff

That's pretty much it for the real needs a vehicle can meet. Of course, there are nuances to these needs, especially with the last two needs. When it comes to transporting other people, some of us simply have to transport ourselves and allow ourselves passenger space for another. Others of us need to transport fairly large groups fairly often. If you have a family of five, it doesn't make much sense to buy a four-passenger vehicle, for example.

Similar logic applies to transporting stuff. The single person who is footloose and fancy-free might not have a need to carry much cargo, so a small hatchback or coupe works just fine. But that same single person might want to transport a canoe on the roof or tote hundreds of pounds of power tools and gear to a job site. Those requirements change the list of possible vehicles that should be considered, well, considerably.

Look at Your Current Vehicle

Choosing a vehicle based on your personal requirements is common sense, and many of us go through this process at least subconsciously before we buy our cars. What most people don't do is use a comparison tool they have readily at hand—their current vehicle. What I suggested to prospective vehicle buyers in *The Complete Idiot's Guide to Buying or Leasing a Car* was simply to sit down with a piece of paper and jot down all the positives and negatives they could think of about the vehicle they were driving. That's still a good idea if only because it gets you thinking clearly about things you'd like and areas in which you'd like to see improvement.

Don't think all these attributes have to be concrete or finite either. If you'd like your next vehicle simply to look better or be more in vogue than your current ride, that's okay. As I said, I'm on to the fact that people buy their cars for a variety of tangible and intangible reasons, so I won't tell on you, and I won't laugh if you want something simply because you want it. A recent study examined the reasons people said they decided to buy a new vehicle, and here they are:

Consumers' top 5 reasons for buying a new vehicle are:

Old car had high mileage	35.2%
Tired of old car, wanted something new	22.0%

Old car was always in for repairs	20.4%
Wanted a car with better gas mileage	19.2%
Old car just died	17.6%

Source: BIGresearch

But please be specific. If you'd like a bigger car or truck, just how much bigger does it need to be? If you want more passenger- or cargo-carrying capacity, define that as best you can. If you need towing capabilities, how heavy is the load you are going to tow?

Because you are reading this book I presume you want better fuel economy but, again, what kind of gains are you looking for? Do you expect the fuel economy increase to give you a quick payback for the added expense you might have to pay to get it? Or are you content that saving fossil fuel is a worthy goal, and you're not looking for a specific payback?

Even more nebulous, but certainly important, is the value you put on making your personal response to key issues such as global warming, clean air, and preservation of natural resources. Each and every one of these issues is worthy of our attention and our good works, but how do you put a price tag on that? As you've seen by the cost analyses in the previous chapters, buying features that allow each of us as individuals to address these major issues of our time has its costs.

Those costs should be recognized, acknowledged, and understood without prejudice. Asking any new technology to provide added benefits over those of old technology, and do it cheaper, is asking a lot. But that is what some are asking of hybrid and alternative fuel technologies. They want them not only to clean the air, help stabilize the climate, and lessen our nation's reliance on foreign petroleum, but they also want them to do it at less cost than conventional gasoline vehicles. That's a tall order and, in my opinion, an unfair expectation.

Looking at your current vehicle should help you hone more realistic expectations. If you pull a horse trailer with your current vehicle, buying a Prius just isn't going to cut it. If you have a big SUV to cart around your family of six, even a hybrid SUV such as the Toyota

Highlander, Ford Escape, or Saturn Vue Green Line isn't going to get the job done. So think about what you need, what you want, and what you're willing to give up.

How Much Driving Do You Do?

One important step is to determine how much driving you do. Clock how far it is back and forth to work. Look at any regular trips you make that could add considerable miles to your monthly total. Throw in a contingency factor of some additional miles, because your life tomorrow won't be exactly what it is today. And when you have all that totaled up, multiply the monthly number by 12 to get a yearly "budget" of miles driven. That's crucial in looking at the economics of a hybrid or alternative fuel vehicle.

What Type of Driving Do You Do?

But just having that miles-driven figure isn't enough. It is almost equally important to determine what kind(s) of driving you do. Are you an outside salesperson who puts several hundred miles on you car each week at freeway speeds? Or are you a dyed-in-the-wool urban commuter who makes the stop-and-go crawl to work 5 days a week? Are most of your miles driven in free-and-easy traffic at relatively high velocities? Or do you mostly drone from stop sign to stoplight? And don't forget who is in the car with you when you travel. Are you most often alone or do you more frequently carry passengers?

Tailor Your Vehicle to Your Driving

Understanding both the amount of driving you do (and plan to do) and the type of driving you do (and plan to do) is essential to making a good decision on what type of hybrid or alternative fuel vehicle to buy. For example, if you do a lot of high-speed interstate driving when traffic is clear, you might think you need a hybrid, but the reality is you, and for that matter the planet, will not see all the advantages from that purchase that you might expect. The reason for that is when a hybrid

Boosters

Clean diesel technology offers the promise of significantly better fuel efficiency—20 to 40 percent better—with excellent exhaust emissions performance.

vehicle is cruising an interstate highway at or near the legal speed limit, it is nothing more or less than a gasoline-powered vehicle with a slightly smaller than normal engine. It will get laudable fuel economy but that fuel economy could be matched or nearly matched by a small conventional gasoline car, and it might be surpassed by a high-tech clean diesel.

To help you find your dream vehicle, let's sum up the advantages of the various technologies we've covered in this book to help you "profile" yourself as a potential owner of a hybrid or alternative fuel car or truck.

In general, hybrid vehicles offer outstanding fuel economy, excellent pollution-reduction results, and help limit greenhouse gas emissions. Because they offer superior benefits in low-speed stop-and-go traffic, they are ideal for those who drive in heavily congested urban areas (such as Tokyo for instance) or engage in rush hour expressway or freeway driving. Their benefits are muffled, but not eliminated, when driven at high speeds on open rural highways or interstates. Two additional pluses—they are high-tech green cool, and some of them qualify for one-up driving in the carpool lane.

The benefits offered by different technology varies. The following list shows what kind of fuel economy improvements result from the use of individual technologies.

Percentage of Fuel Savings by Technology

Engine Technologies

Variable Valve Timing and Lift   Improves engine efficiency by optimizing the flow of fuel and air into the engine for various engine speeds.   **5%**

Cylinder Deactivation   Saves fuel by deactivating cylinders when they are not needed.   **7.5%**

Turbocharger and Supercharger   Increases engine power, allowing manufacturers to downsize engines without sacrificing performance or to increase performance without lowering fuel economy. **7.5%**

Engine Technologies

Integrated Starter/Generator (ISG) System   Automatically turns the engine on/off when the vehicle is stopped to reduce fuel consumed during idling.   **8%**

Direct Fuel Injection (with turbocharging or supercharging)   Delivers higher performance with lower fuel consumption.   **11-13%**

Transmission Technologies

Continuously Variable Transmission (CVTs)   Has an infinite number of "gears," providing seamless acceleration and improved fuel economy.   **6%**

Automated Manual Transmission (AMTs)   Combines the efficiency of manual transmissions with the convenience of automatics (gears shift automatically).   **7%**

Source: United States Department of Energy

Compared to hybrids, Flex Fuel vehicles don't have nearly the cool factor, nor do they offer much in the way of fuel economy benefits. Plus, their possible cost-saving benefits hinge completely on the cost of gasoline versus the cost of E85 where you fill up. However, they do score points on lessening our reliance on foreign oil, because the ethanol that is the bulk of their fuel is homegrown here in the United States. And they are better than conventional gasoline cars in the greenhouse gas emission arena. An additional plus for Flex Fuel vehicles is the fact that they require little or no premium when purchasing a conventional gasoline car and, if need be, they can run on conventional gasoline. Another positive for FFVs is the fact that so many different types of vehicles are available with the capability.

Individuals with long commutes or who make frequent short trips in a localized area are the prime suspects when it comes to owning a natural gas vehicle. Natural gas vehicles are very clean emission-wise; they don't produce as much CO_2 as similar conventional vehicles, and they burn a fuel that is presently abundant here in North America and available from friendly nations around the world. These positives are offset by the hefty premium you have to pay for a natural gas vehicle, which could well negate the potential cost savings realized by using the less-expensive fuel versus gasoline. Right now you have just one choice—a version of the Honda Civic—but the good news is that the car qualifies for one-person use in many carpool lanes. The inconvenience of the lack of natural gas filling stations might be turned into a positive if you like the idea of filling up at home with an appliance installed in your garage.

Diesels offer fuel efficiency bordering on the Environmental Protection Agency (EPA) ratings of the top-ranked hybrids, and they have garnered a reputation for longevity, toughness, and simplicity. This means they have cost benefits, despite the fact that they are often premium-priced versus conventional cars and trucks. On the environmental side, though, the benefits are few unless you use biodiesel or rig your engine to run on vegetable oil.

Today's electric vehicles are strictly for those with short commutes and/ or who do a lot of urban driving. Pure electrics offer excellent benefits on the environmental side because they emit virtually nothing into our air—neither pollutants nor greenhouse gases. They do require electricity generated somewhere and somehow, though, and those generating plants might burn oil, natural gas, or coal (all fossil fuels) and emit carbon dioxide. But there is little debate about electrics being clean, clean, clean. The major downsides are two-fold—limited range on a charge and high expense. For many the limited range is a deal-breaker. The few electrics on the market today are also extremely small with accompanying limited passenger- and cargo-capacity.

Today's Partial Zero Emission Vehicles (PZEVs) bear little initial cost penalty and turn in fuel economy similar to conventional cars of the same size and weight. In terms of limiting conventional exhaust emissions, they are right in the same stellar area as the best of the hybrids. Equally important, they feel similar to conventional gasoline cars.

Vehicles with displacement on demand (DoD) engines also drive similar to conventional cars. A creative way to look at DoD technology is that it offers drivers the choice of two engines within one vehicle. There is a large displacement engine for power, acceleration, and towing ability, and there is a small engine for good fuel economy in over-the-road cruising. Both power plants just happen to be located in the same engine. Most of a displacement on demand engine's benefits in fuel economy come when driven in low-load moderate to high-speed driving on level surfaces and moderate grades. DoD vehicles are just marginally better than conventional engines in exhaust emission performance but, because they burn less fuel, they do help somewhat in greenhouse gas emissions. DoD technology is currently confined to large vehicles so, although they do improve fuel economy versus their conventional counterparts, they certainly don't go for the green the way a hybrid does.

Shades of Gray

The knee-jerk reaction of some of those in the environmental community is that pure electrics are great (and even greater if they run only on wind- or solar-generated power); hybrids are very good; natural gas vehicles are pretty good; Flex Fuel (ethanol) vehicles are a sham; diesels are an air-quality disaster; and displacement on demand vehicles are gas-guzzlers in light makeup.

But as we've seen, the reality is far more complex than that. Pure electrics are essentially nonexistent now, and when they were around many of them got their power from relatively dirty, CO_2-belching generating plants. Sophisticated hybrids such as the Prius do offer startling environmental benefits and great fuel economy, but they are so expensive they haven't entered the automotive mainstream. And other hybrid applications, such as the Honda Accord hybrid or the Lexus 400h SUV, intentionally give up fuel economy and CO_2 emissions to gain better power and performance.

Boosters

In a quest to broaden the appeal of hybrids, Lexus and Honda now offer hybrid-powered vehicles whose strong performance might be as appealing as their fuel economy. More of these "hybrid" hybrids should be on the way.

Although electrics and hybrids have largely ignored downsides, Flex Fuel and clean diesel vehicles have largely ignored upsides. Because Flex Fuel tech is cheap it can be put into the hands of virtually every driver with minimal cost penalties, and it does curb harmful emissions, though, admittedly, not to the extent that a hybrid does. Meanwhile, clean diesel promises to offer emissions performance equal to that of the top gasoline engines while at the same time offering 20 to 40 percent better fuel efficiency. Further, if you switch from petro-diesel to biodiesel, there are exhaust emission and fuel security benefits. Plus you can use your motor fuel on your salad if need be.

Finally, even though DoD vehicles get little or no respect in the environmental community, they do represent an opportunity to save as much as 10 percent of the fuel we are currently using while, at the same time, giving typical Americans vehicles that can tow a boat, tote bails of hay, carry construction materials to a job, or take the family to the lake. If the DoD vehicles are fueled with E85, as some of them can be, there are also exhaust emission and foreign oil issue benefits.

Fuel Economy per Person Transported

Earlier I mentioned that it is important to keep in mind how many people you plan to transport when you go about choosing your next vehicle. There is more to this than simply determining the number of seats you need, too. There is a much-overlooked aspect of the fuel economy and oil consumption issue that revolves around passengers transported. It might be summed up in a statistic called miles per gallon per person (MPGP).

Here's an example to illustrate the premise. Let's take a current model year Toyota Prius, the hybrid vehicle poster child, and the Chevrolet Tahoe, the highest-selling large SUV in the country and a target of some environmental groups. The Prius has an EPA combined mileage rating of 55 mpg, while the Tahoe has a rating of 18 mpg running on gasoline and also, because we have chosen a Flex Fuel example, 13 mpg on E85. So far the Prius offers a big advantage.

But if you look at the MPGP, the Prius commuting in the carpool lane with only the driver aboard has an MPGP of 55, but the Tahoe commuting in the carpool lane with driver and passenger aboard has an MPGP of 26 on E85 and 36 on gasoline. And a Tahoe with a typical load of one mom and three kids has an MPGP of 52 on E85 and 72 on gasoline. So even though the individual driving the Prius might feel a little smug about saving the planet, the mom and her three kids are actually having a similar net effect on petroleum consumption. In fact,

you could make the case that
when using E85 they are doing
more green good getting to their
destination than the one person
in the Prius, because E85 has
a positive impact on our use of
foreign fuel.

Is this a fair comparison? That's
for you to judge. How often do
you see a hybrid such as a Prius
with just one aboard? How often
do you see a full-size SUV such

> **Boosters** _____
>
> To the surprise of most,
> the EPA says the Toyota
> Prius and the Chevrolet
> Tahoe running on E85
> have identical impacts on
> oil consumption on a per-
> vehicle basis. This assumes,
> of course, that the Tahoe
> always uses E85.

as the Tahoe filled with a family? Certainly the above example stacks
the deck in favor of the SUV. To expand on the comparison, the Prius
with a full load of five passengers has an MPGP of 275, while the
Tahoe with a full load of eight passengers has an MPGP of 104 on E85
and 144 on gasoline, far from that of the Prius. This is not intended as
a knock at hybrids, but it is intended to prompt a more analytical look
at how these vehicles are used, who uses them, and how that relates to
your situation.

It also is intended to point out that some of us want and, to some
extent, need SUVs. These are people with large families, who often
engage in outdoor activities, and who need to take gear with them
when they venture out—in short, just the type of salt-of-the-earth
people who are concerned with the environment and issues such as
global warming.

The SUV Conundrum

Some have suggested that owners of SUVs are uncaring, unpatriotic,
or even power-mad. You can judge for yourself whether these are
fair characterizations. I would simply say there are several ways for
Americans to reap the benefits of SUVs while doing their part to help
on crucial issues such as clean air and fossil fuel use.

Hybrid SUVs

One obvious method to achieve all that is to consider a hybrid SUV. Several are now on the market, and each one of them offers approximately a 20 percent advantage in fuel economy versus a similar conventionally powered model. For example, the Toyota Highlander hybrid and Saturn Vue Green Line are rated at a combined 29 mpg by the EPA, while the similar nonhybrid versions are rated at 24 mpg.

Potholes

The auto industry has had high hopes for its gasoline-electric hybrid SUVs, but up to now their sales have been disappointing.

Because its hybrid system is more sophisticated than the Saturn's, the Highlander is better on its EPA air pollution and greenhouse gas scores. On the other hand, the Saturn is significantly less expensive overall, and the premium charged for Saturn's hybrid system is significantly less than Toyota charges for its system.

Flex Fuel SUVs

For those who want more cargo- and passenger-carrying capabilities than even the mid-size Toyota Highlander can deliver, a Flex Fuel full-size SUV such as the GMC Yukon (the twin of the Chevrolet Tahoe) can offer environmental advantages versus the gasoline-only conventional model. Although fuel economy suffers versus the gas vehicle (13 mpg versus 18 mpg combined), the Flex Fuel version offers significant advantages on oil consumption and greenhouse gas emissions. When operated 100 percent of the time on E85, the Yukon will consume 6.2 barrels of petroleum annually, while the conventional Yukon will consume 20.1. The Flex Fuel Yukon will produce 8.4 tons of greenhouse gases versus 10.7 tons by its conventional counterpart.

Displacement on Demand SUVs

Some full-size SUVs also offer DoD technology (called Multi-Displacement System by Chrysler and Active Fuel Management by General Motors). This is a way to get some benefits on fuel consumption, clean air, and global warming issues while not having to find and pay for E85. Using Active Fuel Management, the GMC Yukon and Chevrolet Tahoe achieve an 18 mpg combined rating versus a 17 mpg rating for the conventional model, and a 22 mpg highway rating versus 20 mpg. When just looking at the numbers, the difference hardly seems to matter, but it does represent a significant change, especially when multiplied by hundreds of thousands of SUVs in operation. In terms of oil consumption, EPA rates the conventional vehicle at 20.1 barrels per year versus 19.0 barrels for the DoD vehicle. The AFM Yukon is projected to produce 10.1 tons of greenhouse gases in a year compared to 10.7 tons for the conventional version.

There is no way around the fact that a large vehicle with multiple capabilities such as a full-size SUV will not achieve the fuel economy of a much smaller vehicle such as a Prius or Honda Civic hybrid. Nor will it offer the same performance in exhaust and greenhouse gas emissions. But neither will it offer the fuel economy or environmental benefits of a small gasoline-powered conventional car. The laws of physics just won't allow it. Does that mean none of us should be allowed to drive full-size SUVs? You can be the judge of that.

Hybrids: The Good and the Bad

Taking an analytical look at hybrids, it is my opinion that the popular press praises them unfairly and knocks them unfairly. First, the press praises them for their stellar fuel economy, and there is no doubt that their EPA fuel economy numbers outstrip those of conventional vehicles. But in fairness, hybrids rarely if ever achieve the fuel economy numbers ascribed to them by the EPA in real-world driving. In many instances, real-world fuel economy seems to be similar, though still better, than similar-sized conventional vehicles. The few small diesels in the market can give the hybrids a run for their money in real-world fuel economy, too, but that rarely gets reported.

The popular press also praises hybrids for their environmental benefits, and those are real and very laudable. But it is rarely pointed out that they still burn fossil fuel and they still emit greenhouse gases. They represent positive benefits, but they are not the "silver bullet" that some make them out to be.

On the other hand, I think the knocks on hybrids are more unfair than the misplaced praise. After the first blush of praise for hybrids came the revisionist criticism that they aren't "cost-effective." The big downside, so say hybrid critics, is the "payback period" for reaping the cost benefits of the hybrid system is too long. Well, I ask you, what is the payback period for getting a premium sound system in a luxury sedan? What is the payback period for getting the V8 engine in a sports coupe? What is the payback period for getting an automatic transmission in a small hatchback? The answer, obviously, is that we don't even view the options that way. If we want better sound quality or quicker acceleration or driving ease from our vehicles and we are willing to pay for it, what is the complaint? We shouldn't have to justify it.

That holds even truer with a hybrid because the benefits are much more altruistic. Only the driver benefits from opting for a V8 engine in his sports coupe, but we in the United States and the world at large benefit from the purchase of a hybrid vehicle. Making that choice, even if it costs you money to do it, should be praised, not scoffed at.

The Cheapest Vehicle for You

In this book we have looked at a wide variety of technologies, some new, some old, most new wrinkles on old ideas. Many of them offer better fuel economy than conventional gasoline-powered vehicles, and in this era of high and volatile gasoline prices, that is very appealing. But if your pursuit of knowledge of hybrids and alternative fuel vehicles is all about you saving money you might be disheartened to learn the simple truth—in most instances, the cheapest vehicle for you to drive is the one you own right now. In other words, it is almost always less expensive to go on driving the vehicle you are currently driving than to buy a new vehicle, even though your current vehicle gets poorer gas mileage than a vehicle you might buy to replace it.

Why is this so? The realities of the automobile market. For one thing, the vehicle you own now, even if it was purchased new, is a used car, and it has depreciated in value considerably since you bought it. If you sell it now, you are giving up its remaining useful life at a discounted rate versus what it was worth when new. If you buy a hybrid or alternative fuel vehicle of the same model year as your current car, you can limit this penalty somewhat. (It'll really hit you if you trade your current vehicle for a new one, as many of us do.) But because hybrids and other high-fuel-economy cars have been depreciating at a slower rate than conventional vehicles, you're still going to lose money. Further, it costs money to switch vehicles. There are sales taxes and licensing fees to be dealt with. You also might want a certified mechanic to look over the used car before you buy it, and that costs as well.

There are only two instances when adhering to a "keep-and-maintain" philosophy fails in comparison to trading for something new. First, if you're getting a new vehicle no matter what. If that's the case you should look to get one with better fuel economy and better emissions. Second, if your current vehicle is in such deplorable condition that it cannot be repaired and maintained in any kind of cost-effective manner. Again, if this is the case why not try to replace it with a clean, fuel-thrifty vehicle?

Which Hybrid or Alternative Fuel Vehicle Is Best?

As a guy who has been testing and reviewing automobiles for the better part of a quarter century, I'm often asked pointblank, "What car should I buy?" I wish I had a one-size-fits-all answer to that question because it would sure save time. But as I tell the callers to my radio show, "America on the Road," it all depends on your individual circumstances, plus your needs and desires. Cars, trucks, minivans, and SUVs are complex products with a number of attributes, some good, some bad. Expecting the same type of vehicle to fill every person's needs and wants is naïve.

What I hope this book has done is give you the analytical tools and the perspective to make your own good decision. The exciting news is, after years and years of cars with similar powertrains, the vehicles of today offer unprecedented choice, and the future holds the hope of even more choices and even more effective technology.

No matter what type of vehicle you decide to buy—hybrid, Flex Fuel, clean diesel, natural gas, pure electric, or new tech gasoline—I hope you will take the important issues that we have returned to again and again in this book into account when you make your next purchase. I'm not asking you to bear the weight of the environmental movement on your shoulders, but I am asking you to consider vehicles that will make the situation better rather than worse. The future of our children and of our planet depends on that.

The Least You Need to Know

- Before you can make the right vehicle choice you have to take stock of your needs and desires.

- When looking at possible choices try to "profile" yourself and then match that profile to the type of vehicle that best fits your criteria. It's okay to be you.

- SUVs have been demonized by some, but when they are carrying a full load of passengers they actually offer decent fuel efficiency. New technologies such as hybrid, Flex Fuel, and DoD, however, can offer serious improvements without sacrificing usability.

- Your least-expensive vehicle choice is to continue to drive the vehicle you're presently driving, but improving the quality of our air and lessening our use of fossil fuels from politically unstable countries are benefits we should be willing to pay for.

Chapter 12

Coming Attractions

In This Chapter

- Finding hydrogen in your future
- Varying mildly and wildly on the hybrid theme
- Seeking the magic bullet
- Filling 'er up with hydrogen

These days we hear a great deal about the "hydrogen economy," and many think that hydrogen is the future. There is a groundswell of predictions that it will be the fuel that will relieve us of having to worry about petroleum and where we're going to get it. Hydrogen is everywhere. On the automotive front, the natural corollary of that notion is the expectation we will move from internal combustion-powered vehicles, which include hybrids, to hydrogen fuel-cell vehicles. Fuel cells powered the Lunar Rover and the robot devices that explored Mars, so why not have one in your own driveway? But those closest to fuel-cell research, especially as it concerns automotive transport, say we are a long way—perhaps decades—from seeing practical fuel-cell-powered vehicles for consumers. Meanwhile you have to get to work and get the kids to school.

So what are the short-term answers to the questions of high fuel prices and dirty air that haven't made it to the public yet? And what are the technologies we might see way down the road somewhere? Although gasoline-electric hybrids, Flex Fuel, and natural gas vehicles are already on the market, among the competing technologies that show promise in the fuel economy and environmental arena are so-called "mild" hybrids, plug-in hybrids, and diesel-electric hybrids. Each of these three types of vehicles could be ready for consumer purchase relatively soon. Depending on the cost of petroleum, we also may see an expanded use of ethanol, *methanol*, natural gas, and biodiesel, and there is no reason that hybrids can't be powered by those alternative fuels.

> **? Definitions**
>
> **Methanol** is an alcohol fuel similar to ethanol but primarily produced by a process using natural gas as the basic component. That has limited its appeal, but the prospect of producing methanol from nonpetroleum sources such as coal or biomass could breathe new life into it.

The more distant future might see hydrogen fuel-cell vehicles and hydrogen-powered internal combustion engine cars. A breakthrough in battery technology might also lead to a resurgence and eventual dominance of electric vehicles in their third major go-round in the marketplace. Each vehicle type has its proponents and detractors, and each has its pluses and minuses but, as this is being written, it is unclear which of these technologies will take its place among the mainstream vehicle propulsion technologies. It is even more difficult to predict which, if any, of these will become dominant in the next decade and into the future. What we do know is that all these technologies could be available for consumer purchase by the year 2020.

The Nearer Future

More extreme and less extreme. Confusingly, those are the two directions gasoline-electric hybrid technology is heading over the next few years. The move to more extreme hybrids is represented by what are being called "plug-in hybrids," while the trend toward less extreme hybrids is represented by vehicles termed "mild" or "partial" hybrids. Although the key goal of the former is to get even more environmental and fuel economy benefits than are available with today's hybrids, the goal of the latter is to put hybrids into more people's garages by removing some of the costs.

Mild or Partial Hybrids

To a lot of consumers a hybrid is a hybrid is a hybrid. "A hybrid will save me money on gas, and they all work about the same, so don't bother me with the details," many consumers say. Well, we hate to break it to you, but you should be bothered about the details. Though in the beginning hybrid technology from the various manufacturers ran in parallel paths, the technology has now started to go different ways. One way is toward performance, and thus we have seen cars such as the Lexus GS 450h, a fun-to-drive sedan that is the fastest member of the sporty GS line. Another way is toward making hybrid technology more affordable, a philosophy that has led to what are being referred to as "mild" or "partial" hybrids.

Frankly, in the world of auto journalists and in the hybrid community, mild hybrids don't get much respect. They don't deliver the huge fuel economy increases the so-called "full" hybrids do, and the decreases they promise in exhaust emissions and greenhouse gases aren't nearly as eye-popping either. But you have to ask the question: is the world better served by highly technical and expensive hybrids owned by a relative few or by less technical and less-expensive hybrids owned by many more? Yes, the more sophisticated hybrids will drink less fuel and spew fewer emissions, but weigh that against the overall effects of having somewhat less-effective hybrids in more hands and you might find new respect for mild hybrids.

One of the leading lights of the partial hybrid movement is the Saturn Vue Green Line sport utility vehicle. Its "belt alternator starter hybrid" is uncomplicated and easy to implement on any number of vehicles, versus the much more complicated integrated hybrid system of the Toyota Prius or Honda Civic Hybrid.

Among the advantages of the belt alternator starter hybrid (its long name not being one of them) is the fact that it can be applied to multiple engines with minimal changes to the engine or transmission. For example, in the Saturn Vue Green Line, the system is mated to a 2.4-liter four-cylinder engine and an electronically controlled automatic transmission. Because of this, the system eschews the advantage of using a smaller-than-standard engine, but the use of an engine and transmission that would otherwise power the car has benefit on the cost side by removing added complexity. And the system does improve fuel economy by using typical hybrid techniques such as automatic engine start-shutoff, early fuel cutoff during deceleration, battery charging during deceleration, and "intelligent" battery charging.

Also, as with a more sophisticated hybrid, the belt alternator starter hybrid provides electric-motor power assist during acceleration when needed. During a wide-open throttle maneuver, the system uses the alternator/motor to supplement the engine's torque. Rather than integrating the electric motor with the transmission, the system uses an *aramid* cord belt that transmits motor torque to the crankshaft when needed for acceleration and from the crankshaft to the alternator to generate electricity to charge the nickel-metal hydride battery pack.

> **Definitions**
>
> **Aramid** is a strong, fire-resistant synthetic fiber often used to reinforce or strengthen other materials. Kevlar and Nomex are trade-named aramids.

In the motoring mode, the belt alternator starter hybrid is used to quickly restart the engine upon brake pedal release and to provide momentary acceleration assist as needed. The hybrid's power electronics convert the electrical energy to run the motor/generator unit as a motor. In the generating mode, the system is used to provide both 12-volt vehicle power for accessories such as radio and heater fan and power to recharge the hybrid battery. To perform these functions, the engine is used to power the motor/generator unit, which then provides an electrical output. In this mode, the energy may come from either gasoline when accelerating or the kinetic energy of the moving vehicle when decelerating with the fuel cut off.

According to EPA estimates, the partial hybrid in the Saturn Vue Green Line SUV will result in 23 percent better fuel economy in city driving and 19 percent better fuel economy on the highway. These figures do not represent the startling gains seen by the hybrid systems from Honda or Toyota, but the premium being asked for the GM system is roughly half the 20 percent additional cost being asked for the Japanese hybrids versus their conventional equivalents. In addition, the Vue Green Line's hybrid powertrain is more powerful than the powertrain in the comparable four-cylinder version of the vehicle.

In addition to General Motors, DaimlerChrysler is another major global player that has advocated the use of "milder" hybrids. Because such systems are far less complex to develop, engineer, and manufacture, they can be much more palatably priced than the so-called "full hybrid" systems. Because of this, even Toyota, an acknowledged leader in full hybrids, has been reported to be eyeballing milder hybrid systems in an effort to reach its goal of selling 1 million hybrid vehicles by 2020.

Plug-In Hybrids

If systems similar to the belt alternator starter hybrid represent the mild side of the future of transportation, the plug-in hybrid represents the wild side. Although the mild hybrids also offer relatively mild benefits in fuel mileage and gas emissions, the plug-in hybrid (PHEV) concept offers benefits in those areas that make today's hybrids pale in comparison.

The big difference between a plug-in hybrid and the hybrids on the road today is, well, you plug it in. We're sure you grasped that, but you might not grasp the why, because you know hybrids carry their own electrical generating capacity and are much more convenient than electric cars because you don't have to plug them in. But plug-in hybrids take that potential negative and turn it into a positive by using extra battery capacity charged by your electrical connection at home—"the grid"—to give the vehicle extended range in all-electric mode. When vehicles run in all-electric mode they emit zero emissions, and they get incredible fuel economy. For instance, a Toyota Prius that has been equipped with large-format lithium-ion batteries and a new integrated control system is claimed to be capable of 180 miles-per-gallon for 60-mile urban commutes. That's about three times the economy of today's

Prius. Why? Because at 33 mph and under the vehicle operates in electric-only mode.

The added battery capacity allows significant amounts of zero-emission driving with PHEVs. This addresses one of the unheralded issues with current hybrids, namely they still use fossil fuel and still emit quantities of internal combustion engine exhaust and so-called greenhouse gases. Because of the stellar fuel economy, PHEVs also offer incredible range, which means fewer trips to the gas station.

If the out-of-this-world fuel economy and incredible range aren't mind-boggling enough, there also is talk about developing a "vehicle-to-grid" plug-in hybrid, which would not only take power from the electrical grid but also actually provide power to the grid when it had an excess. How's this scenario work? Say you arrive home and your PHEV's batteries are topped off, those batteries could power your TV and your refrigerator for a period of time until the vehicle controller signaled them to cease providing electricity. At that point your home would shift to power from the grid, and the PHEV would go dormant. Hours later it would draw in power to top off its batteries again before you head to work the next day.

Not all these benefits come free though. Plug-in hybrids do use some electricity that is not created by their on-board generating system or regenerative braking, and that electricity might well be produced by coal-fired generating stations. Those plants create greenhouse gases and other pollution, but many experts think those emissions would be easier to clean up than emissions from millions of motor vehicles. The major issue with plug-in hybrids is one of expense. In fact, the larger battery packs they require would be much more expensive than the battery packs carried by today's hybrids.

Diesel and Alt-Fuel Hybrids

As we have discussed, a hybrid vehicle is simply a vehicle that uses two sources of motive power. These days all the hybrids that come from major manufacturers use gasoline-powered engines in combination with an electric motor, but there is no reason the engine has to be fueled with gasoline. The batteries and the electric motor really don't care what kind of engine keeps them fully charged with electricity, so diesel, biodiesel, ethanol, and natural gas engines are logical candidates for future hybrids.

In fact the Europeans, who are at the forefront of diesel technology, have already announced diesel-hybrid prototypes and are hopeful of gaining traction with them. They will most likely appear first in Europe, because United States regulators still don't know quite what to do about the clean-diesel technology we discussed in Chapter 7. That's a shame because the efficiency of a diesel engine combined with a sophisticated hybrid drivetrain could result in record-setting fuel efficiency and minimal levels of greenhouse gas production. And if the regulators approved the use of urea-based NOX mitigation, the exhaust emissions would be very clean as well. Diesel hybrids will benefit from the fact that a diesel fuel infrastructure is already in place. Biodiesel could, of course, use the same delivery methods to get into consumers' vehicles.

The odds against ethanol and natural gas hybrids are longer. The knock on ethanol is that its environmental benefits versus gasoline aren't that great. The problem for natural gas hybrids is two-fold. First, there is no consumer-friendly fuel delivery infrastructure for natural gas in the United States. Second, the combination of a big natural gas pressure tank and heavy batteries presents what auto engineers call a "packaging problem." In other words it will be hard to fit both into a practical car.

Beyond the Near Future

When most experts look over the horizon to the types of fuels we might be using in 50 years, they return with one of two answers. Some predict that we will be using the same fuels we are using today, gasoline and diesel from petroleum supplemented by ethanol, biodiesel, and other renewable fuels. Hybrids of all types—mild, full, plug-in, and diesel—fit into this scenario as well. Others answer with a single word—hydrogen.

Hydrogen Fuel-Cell Vehicles

It seems similar to the proverbial magic bullet. Imagine if you will an energy source that leaves no residue except some water and a bit of carbon dioxide. Unlike an internal combustion engine, it doesn't produce particulates, nitrous oxides, carbon monoxide, or anything else that might cause damage to our air or our bodies. All this is possible because, unlike the typical gasoline or diesel automobile engine, the fuel cell doesn't use combustion to create power. Instead it uses a simple chemical reaction to make electricity, which can then be used to power electric motors, electronic equipment, or stored in batteries for future use.

If all this seems too good to be true, here's a fact: fuel cells have been used in the United States space program since the 1960s. So why hasn't the auto industry jumped on this technology long before now? Well, actually the industry has toyed with fuel cells for decades, but only in the last 15 years, spurred by having to market zero-emissions vehicles mandated by law, has the industry become serious about employing fuel-cell technology. Now major players such as General Motors, Ford Motor Company, Toyota, and DaimlerChrysler are working overtime to bring fuel-cell vehicles to the market.

> **Boosters**
>
> Fuel cells are so reliable that today they are used to provide power for out-of-the-way hotels and hospitals that find it too expensive to tap into traditional electric power grids.

As to a fuel cell itself, it's somewhat synonymous with a storage battery that doesn't require recharging. Similar to a battery, it consists of two electrodes around an electrolyte. Oxygen passes over one electrode and a fuel, hydrogen, passes over the other, resulting in a chemical reaction that creates a flow of electrons (electricity), heat, and a hydrogen-oxygen combination commonly called "water." Unlike batteries that "run down" after continuous discharge, fuel cells will continue to make electricity, heat, and water as long as they are provided with oxygen and hydrogen. Unlike the typical vehicle engine, which converts energy stored in its fuel to usable power via combustion (i.e., burning), fuel cells chemically combine the molecules of a fuel and an oxidizer without burning, dispensing with the inefficiencies and pollution of traditional combustion.

In an era of constant tradeoffs, there seems to be nothing but an upside for fuel-cell technology. But before you start whistling show tunes as you skip off merrily through a field of daisies, the technology does present challenges. Perhaps the biggest challenge is the capture and handling of the volatile element hydrogen. As proved in the grainy film footage of the explosion of the dirigible Hindenburg, hydrogen gas is explosive. Given this, one trick that must be mastered in developing fuel cells that will work in vehicle applications is finding effective and safe ways of refueling with hydrogen. Various methods have been tried, including cold storage of liquid hydrogen and assorted methods of storing hydrogen gas. One of them might be the long-term solution, but the most promising for real-world use in the near-future seems to be, ironically, the gasoline station on the corner. Gasoline as well as other fuels can be broken down to produce hydrogen, which can then be used in fuel cells.

Producing hydrogen from gasoline (or methanol or ethanol) is the job of a "reformer." The reformer is sort of an on-board *cracking* plant that separates hydrogen, which is a component of gasoline, from its other components. Of course, the use of an on-board reformer adds a great deal of complexity (and cost) to each fuel-cell application. Further, building reformers that are compact enough for automotive use is problematical right now, though fuel-cell advocates predict that obstacle soon will be conquered.

Even given the obstacles, reformer-fuel-cell technology seems to be one way to get the technology into practical automobiles relatively quickly. Why? Without reformers, a whole new fuel delivery infrastructure

> **? Definitions**
>
> **Cracking** is a process in which complex organic molecules such as hydrocarbons are converted to the simpler molecules of lighter hydrocarbons. An oil refinery, for example, cracks heavy crude into gasoline, liquid petroleum gas, and other products.

would have to be created from scratch, and the costs of such an undertaking are staggering. Also staggering are the cost of today's fuel cells, but carmakers are hopeful of getting those costs down (way down) to offer vehicles at costs that will be acceptable to consumers.

Despite the huge technical challenges, global car manufacturers say fuel-cell technology is coming. The big question is when. There are fuel-cell vehicles on the road today, and I have driven some of the best of them, including the experimental Honda FCX, which is likely to be the first "production" fuel-cell vehicle on the market. But despite that, it is unlikely we will see them on the road in any appreciable numbers until at least 2020.

Hydrogen-Powered Internal Combustion Cars

Even though fuel-cell vehicles are a decade or two away, for at least one type of hydrogen-fueled vehicle the future is now. BMW, one of several automakers laboring to create hydrogen-fueled vehicles, says it is ready to lease a limited number of hydrogen-powered cars to well-heeled customers. But the cars are not powered by fuel cells. Instead, they use otherwise conventional 12-cylinder BMW engines adapted to accept hydrogen or gasoline. The novel Flex Fuel arrangement is prompted by the lack of hydrogen filling stations. Thus the cars can run on gasoline in a pinch.

What's remarkable about BMW's hydrogen car is how unremarkable it is to drive. The BMW 7 Series Hydrogen 7 Saloon accelerates from 0 to 62 mph in 9.5 seconds, and its top speed is limited electronically to about 140 mph. Although you might think such a vehicle would be very exotic, the truth is it seems so similar to a current BMW luxury sedan that it is hard to tell them apart. Running on hydrogen, the 12-cylinder engine delivers 260 horsepower, and the biggest difference between the hydrogen engine and a conventional BMW 12-cylinder is the intake system that features additional injection valves for the hydrogen. It has a range of more than 200 miles on a hydrogen fill-up.

Assembling an engine that could operate on both gasoline and hydrogen was only part of the task of getting a hydrogen vehicle on the road. Engineers might tell you it was not the most difficult part. Instead, extracting hydrogen, storing it in the vehicle and finding safe methods of fueling the car all were highly difficult challenges.

The most exotic aspect of the car might well be its "Cryo" fuel tank. The hydrogen is stored cryogenically (in super-chilled and liquid form) at minus 250° Celsius in a double-walled steel tank behind the rear seatbacks. Two safety valves ensure controlled ventilation in case of excess pressure. Because hydrogen can be extremely volatile, engineers work long hours ensuring that the storage system is safe. Numerous crash tests have shown that even in the case of a massive rear-end collision, the tank's steel cylinder with its double walls will not leak.

Not leaving anything to chance, the BMW engineers say the tank cannot explode even in very severe crashes "that would leave very little chance for occupant survival." For an explosion to occur, they assure us, hydrogen and air would have to mix, but due to the higher inner pressure of the hydrogen, air cannot enter the tank. We'll take their word on that.

Getting Hydrogen

A major issue with the prediction of a hydrogen-based economy is the vexing problem of obtaining it in forms that can be used as fuel. Like pretty girls, hydrogen is everywhere, but just try getting it alone. In nature, hydrogen is the most abundant substance on Earth, but it is almost always found with something else. The simplest element, hydrogen combines readily with other elements and is almost always found as part of some other substance, such as water, hydrocarbons, or alcohols. It also is found in biomass, which includes you, me, and all plants and animals. To be used as a fuel, it must be derived from compounds that contain it.

> **Potholes**
>
> For the last several decades hydrogen has been the key component of rocket fuel so getting it and storing it is literally rocket science.

Still, many experts, including those at the Department of Energy (DOE), are bullish on hydrogen. They note hydrogen can be produced via various process technologies, including thermal (such as natural gas or gasoline reforming), renewable liquid and bio-oil processing, and biomass and coal gasification. It can even be derived from water using the electrolytic process (which requires the use of external energy sources) or even the photolytic process, which "splits" water using sunlight in conjunction with biological and electrochemical materials.

The key item to note here is that hydrogen doesn't come for free even though it is all around us. It does require energy to derive it from one of the many compounds in which it occurs. There is even some question if the amount of energy contained in hydrogen will outweigh the amount of energy used to derive it. For this reason, energy-efficient methods of obtaining hydrogen are currently much sought-after.

New technology can allow us to capture hydrogen from a wide variety of materials and substances, including trash. A company called Startech has demonstrated what it calls plasma waste remediation and recycling technology. In the process, waste materials continuously fed into the system are safely and economically destroyed, reformed, and recovered by the molecular dissociation and closed-loop elemental recycling process. (Yeah, right.)

Here's how it works: in an atmosphere of ionized air, waste materials are subjected to an intense jolt of energy that is so great it causes their molecules to break apart into actual atoms. (That's the destruction part.) But in addition to reducing waste to atoms, essentially blowing it to bits, the byproduct is plasma converted gas (PCG) from which hydrogen can be readily derived. To prove the concept, Startech has a hydrogen-powered Ford pickup truck running around its plant.

For hydrogen to achieve the destiny that many have predicted for it, two things need to happen. First, hydrogen in usable form must be cost-competitive with the available alternatives that could be used as fuel. In the light-duty vehicle transportation market, DOE figures this means that hydrogen needs to be available at $2 to $3 per gasoline-gallon-equivalency before taxes. This would result in hydrogen fuel-cell vehicles having the same cost to the consumer on a cost-per-mile driven basis as a comparable conventional internal combustion engine or hybrid vehicle. Second, and more problematic, the United States and the world's industrial economies would have to build a hydrogen storage and delivery infrastructure that could service the millions of vehicles that could potentially use hydrogen as fuel. The size of that task is enormous and the costs to execute are almost impossible to calculate. Unlike gasoline, which is pretty happy being stored in a simple tank and delivery truck, hydrogen needs special handling. That means expense.

Even though it is optimistic about hydrogen, the DOE doesn't predict that we will see it available in cost-competitive form until at least 2015 and, it says, other efforts won't come on-stream until after 2030.

The Takeaway

The good news about the future of personal transportation is that the world is filled with very smart, very dedicated people who are working diligently to find solutions to the current problems of high fuel prices, the wasteful use of our fossil fuels and other natural resources, and the issues of air quality and climate change. The solutions exist, quite possibly in technologies we have already identified and are researching.

Some of the technologies described in this book will fall by the wayside. The universal search for efficiency and better answers will weed out those answers that aren't quite good enough for the times. But that search also will provide us with real solutions.

Importantly, arriving at those real solutions requires that people of goodwill agree to goals that look beyond the current generation to the future of the planet and the people who populate it. I'm convinced those answers can be found, and we can make way for tomorrows that include cleaner skies and healthier children.

The Least You Need to Know

- The near future will include deviations on the hybrid theme such as mild hybrids that are less expensive and plug-in hybrids that offer greater savings in fuel and lower emissions.

- Hybrid technology also lends itself to the use of alternative fuels, so future hybrids could burn biodiesel, ethanol, natural gas, or methanol.

◆ Plug-in hybrid vehicles (PHEVs) will offer phenomenal fuel economy and anti-pollution benefits, because they offer many of the advantages of pure electrics.

◆ Fuel cells can be the "magic bullet" when it comes to solving problems such as fossil fuel depletion and greenhouse gas production because the process they use to create electricity results in emissions of harmless water vapor.

◆ Although fuel cells are a longer-term solution for using abundant hydrogen as fuel, a shorter-term solution is using otherwise conventional vehicles that can burn both hydrogen and gasoline.

Appendix A

Comparing the Technologies

This book is packed with information about various automotive technologies. Many are available now; others are expected to become available in the future. The table at the end of this appendix displays quantifiable data about each vehicle type in a single place so you can make easy comparisons. As you compare technologies, note the following:

◆ For currently available vehicles, this table presents ranges of values or individual values that are most representative of each type of vehicle. For future vehicles, the data presents a best-guess about what those values are likely to be. In areas where it is impossible to give a realistic guess because the data is too speculative, I have simply left them blank.

◆ The Initial Cost ranges are self-explanatory. They represent typical purchase prices.

◆ Fuel Economy represents the range of EPA-combined mileage figures for each vehicle type. In cases where no such vehicle has been EPA-certified, the values represent estimates of what that EPA-combined fuel economy range could be.

◆ Range represents miles that can be driven on a full fuel tank or with a full battery charge and utilizes EPA fuel economy estimates.

◆ Passengers represent the maximum number of passengers (including the driver) that can be accommodated by the vehicle in each class with the most seating capacity. (As you might guess, the minimum capacity is one, the loneliest number.)

◆ Towing represents the maximum figure for the vehicle with the highest towing capacity among all in its type. It is expressed in pounds.

◆ Projected Reliability is drawn from several data sources that track vehicle reliability, including *Kelley Blue Book* and J.D. Power and Associates, but represents my own opinion on the issue. It is based on a 5-point scale, ranging from best to worst expressed as Excellent, Very Good, Good, Fair, and Poor.

◆ Projected Resale value is drawn from several data sources that track residual value and related information, including *Kelley Blue Book*, but it represents my own opinion. It is based on the same 5-point scale: Excellent, Very Good, Good, Fair, and Poor.

◆ Projected Ownership Cost also is derived from several data sources, including *Kelley Blue Book* and IntelliChoice, but again, it represents my own opinion. It uses the same 5-point scale.

	Initial Cost	Fuel Economy	Range	Passengers	Towing	Projected Reliability	Projected Resale	Projected Ownership cost
Hybrid Electric	$22–60K	25–60	400–500	7	3500	Excellent	Excellent	Excellent
Flex Fuel	$18–60K	15–30	300–400	8	7700	Very Good	Very Good	Good
Clean Diesel	$40–80K	20–50	400–450	7	2000	Very Good	Very Good	Very Good
Natural Gas	$25–30K	25–45	180–230	5	Not rated	Excellent	Very Good	Excellent
Multi-Displacement	$20–60K	18–30	300–400	8	7700	Very Good	Very Good	Good
Electric	$15–100K	80–120	50–120	4	Not rated	Very Good	Good	Very Good
Plug-In Hybrid	$35–100K	50–100	400–600	7	Not rated			
Mild Hybrid	$22–35K	25–40	300–350	5	1500	Very Good	Good	Fair
Fuel-Cell	$100K+	100+	250–300	5	Not rated			
Hydrogen IC	$100K+	18–30	200–250	5	Not rated	Excellent	Very Good	Fair

Appendix B

Information Resources

As they once said in *The X Files*, the truth is out there. The following resources, many of them available for free on the Internet, are filled with information on hybrid and alternative fuel vehicles.

California Air Resources Board
www.arb.ca.gov
The official website of the powerful and influential California air quality regulatory body.

Commuter Cars
www.commutercars.com
Electric vehicle manufacturer that builds and markets small cars suitable for urban use.

Drive Clean California
www.driveclean.ca.gov
California state information service for environmental issues related to driving.

Electric Auto Association
www.eaaev.org
Nonprofit association designed to promote electric vehicles through information.

Electric Drive Transportation Association
www.electricdrive.org
An industry association dedicated to advancing electric drive as a core
technology for sustainable mobility.

Energy Information Administration
www.eia.doe.gov
The official energy statistics agency of the United States government.

Environmental Protection Agency
www.epa.gov/autoemissions
Source of comparative vehicle data on the basis of fuel economy and
environmental impact.

EV World
www.evworld.com
Commercial site covering the world of electric and alternative fuel
vehicles.

FlexTek
www.flextek.com/index.htm
Company that specializes in the conversion of conventional vehicles
into Flex Fuel capability.

Greasecar
http://greasecar.com
Source for conversion of diesel vehicles to vegetable oil power.

Green Car Congress
www.greencarcongress.com
Commercial site devoted to providing information about various technologies in the quest for sustainable mobility.

Green Car Journal
www.greencar.com
Commercial print and online magazine covering the world of environmental vehicles—edited by auto industry veteran journalist Ron Cogan.

HybridCars.com
www.hybridcars.com
Commercial site covering the gamut of issues relating to hybrid vehicles.

Kelley Blue Book
www.kbb.com
Number one source of automotive information, including vehicle
reviews, pricing, options, and buying tips.

Myers Motors
www.myersmotors.com
Electric vehicle manufacturer with information on purchasing new and
used electric vehicles.

Turbine Car
www.turbinecar.com
Private site with resources and information on Chrysler and other
turbine-powerplant vehicles.

United States Business Council for Sustainable Development
www.usbcsd.org
A nonprofit association of businesses whose purpose is to create and
deliver value-driven, sustainable development projects in the United
States.

United States Department of Energy
www.fueleconomy.gov
Source of information on fuel economy and related issues, including
alternative fuels and hybrid vehicles.

United States Department of Energy Clean Cities Program
www.eere.energy.gov/cleancities
The mission of the Clean Cities Program is to advance the nation's
economic, environmental, and energy security by contributing to the
reduction of petroleum consumption.

The Wilson Quarterly
www.wilsoncenter.org
The official magazine of the Woodrow Wilson International Center for
Scholars, its archives offer insight into the global warming issue.

World Business Council for Sustainable Development
www.wbcsd.org
A group of 180 international companies committed to sustainable
development through economic growth, ecological balance, and social
progress.

Appendix C

Glossary of Hybrid and Alt-Fuel-Related Terms

biodiesel   A fuel that is domestically produced and renewable. It can be made from vegetable oils, animal fats, or recycled restaurant greases. Biodiesel is biodegradable and reduces pollutants such as particulates and carbon monoxide.

biogas   A slang term, similar to biodiesel, covering the variations of methane that go under the aliases swamp gas, marsh gas, and digester gas.

BTL (biomass to liquid)   Synthetic fuels that can be produced by any type of biomass.

carbon-dioxide neutrality   Neither adding nor subtracting carbon dioxide from the environment. Biofuels are said to offer carbon dioxide neutrality because the CO_2 released into the environment by their use was in the environment previously.

cetane number   Also called cetane rating, it is the measure of combustibility under pressure used as a relative measure to rank diesel fuels, which use compression ignition.

cracking   A process in which complex organic molecules such as hydrocarbons are converted to the simpler molecules of lighter hydrocarbons. An oil refinery "cracks" heavy crude into gasoline, liquid petroleum gas, and other products.

energy medium   A substance that contains releasable energy. Examples include coal, natural gas, and petroleum.

evaporative emissions   Gaseous discharges emanating from the fuel system and from the process of filling your gas tank. A vehicle with no evaporative emissions typically has fewer emissions while being driven than a typical gasoline car has while standing still.

fuel cell   Power unit in which hydrogen and oxygen are subjected to a controlled reaction to produce electrical energy. This reaction also generates heat and produces water vapor.

greenhouse effect   A scientific theory that carbon dioxide traps heat in the atmosphere in much the same way as glass in a greenhouse roof does; heat can get in but it can't get out. Some say this is a cause of global warming.

greenhouse gases   Gases including methane, water vapor, chlorofluorocarbons, and carbon dioxide that trap heat in the atmosphere in much the same way as glass in a greenhouse roof does.

GTL (gas to liquid)   Synthetic liquid fuels derived from natural gas. GTL diesel fuel contains neither sulfur nor aromatic hydrocarbons.

homogenous combustion   In a diesel engine, the even distribution of fuel and air in the combustion chamber gives rise to an even temperature distribution, preventing oxides of nitrogen and soot particles from being produced.

hybrid   The combination of two or more independent propulsion units. For example, by using an electric motor as a generator alongside an internal combustion engine, energy can be recovered during the vehicle's braking and deceleration phases and temporarily stored in the battery. In traffic with frequent stops and starts, this can bring considerable savings in fuel consumption.

hydrogen   One of the most prevalent elements on Earth, hydrogen is the energy medium for fuel cell vehicles. It can be obtained on a largely

CO_2-neutral basis from renewable energy sources, but it rarely exists in nature as an isolated substance. Instead it is usually combined with other elements such as water, also known as H_2O.

injectors   Powerful valves actuated to regulate the introduction of fuel in each combustion chamber of an internal combustion engine.

lubricity   The measure of the ability of a liquid to limit friction and wear when introduced between two surfaces.

methanol   An alcohol fuel similar to ethanol but primarily produced by a process using natural gas as the basic component. The prospect of producing methanol from nonpetroleum sources such as coal or biomass exists.

Organization of the Petroleum Exporting Countries (OPEC)   An international organization made up of Algeria, Indonesia, Iran, Iraq, Kuwait, Libya, Nigeria, Qatar, Saudi Arabia, the United Arab Emirates, and Venezuela. This organization deals with oil production and price issues in ways meant to serve its member countries.

ping   The explosion rather than burning of the air-fuel mixture in the combustion chamber of an internal combustion engine. Also called knock, ping can damage your engine, sometimes making holes in the piston.

possible reserves   Oil the oil industry believes has a chance of being developed under "favorable circumstances," often revolving around its location and the current market price of oil. The higher the price, the more favorable the chances of the industry developing oil.

probable reserves   Oil the oil industry believes is "reasonably probable" of being produced using current or soon-to-be-developed technology at current market prices, with the acknowledged consent of the governments involved.

proven reserves   Oil the oil industry believes is "reasonably certain" of being produced using current technology and at current market prices with the acknowledged consent of the governments involved.

pure electric vehicle   A vehicle that uses on-board sources of electricity stored in a battery or battery bank as power. It must be plugged into a source of electricity to recharge its batteries. It is also known as a battery electric vehicle or BEV.

renewable energy   Regenerative energy sources from wind, hydro-electric, geothermic or solar heat power stations, solar cells, and bio-mass.

Super Ultra Low Emission Vehicles (SULEVs)   As defined by the California Air Resources Board, vehicles that are 90 percent cleaner than the average new-model-year car, which means 90 percent cleaner than vehicles that meet federal clean air standards.

turbocharging   A method of enhancing the performance of internal combustion engines by adding compressed air to the combustion chamber. In such an engine an auxiliary compressor ("turbocharger") compresses air so that the engine is supplied with a greater mass of air. At the same time, the amount of fuel supplied to the engine also is increased commensurate with the airflow.

ultra-low sulfur diesel   Diesel fuel that contains far less of the potentially hazardous substance sulfur than does typical American diesel fuel. Sulfur is not only a pollutant, but can also foul and clog catalytic converters and particulate filters meant to deal with other pollutants.

valvetrain   The collection of valves and their associated mechanical and hydraulic operating mechanisms that allow an internal combustion engine to ingest air and expel exhaust gases.

Appendix D

Guide to Current Hybrid and Alternative Fuel Models

The automotive world is ever-changing. Models go into production and out of production on a frequent basis, but the accompanying chart is a comprehensive look at the hybrid and alternative fuel vehicles available on the market today. More, of course, are coming as auto manufacturers from around the world try to tap into consumers' desires for better fuel economy, lower emissions, and less consumption of precious fossil fuels. Because of this, it is expected that in the coming months you will have more hybrid, displacement-on-demand, and clean diesel models to choose from. The future also might hold consumer-available diesel-electric hybrids, plug-in hybrids, and fuel cell vehicles.

The chart is largely self-explanatory, but following are some important notes:

◆ Flex Fuel indicates the vehicle is powered by an internal combustion engine that can use gasoline or E85.

◆ MDAF is shorthand for multi-displacement active-fuel management. These displacement-on-demand systems allow eight-cylinder engines to use just four cylinders in low-load situations, saving fuel. As you'll see in the following chart, some displacement-on-demand systems also include Flex Fuel capability.

◆ Gas-elec hybrid is short for gasoline-electric hybrid.

◆ Natural gas means the vehicle can be operated only on natural gas. Some previous natural gas systems also could switch over to gasoline, an earlier type of Flex Fuel system.

◆ Clean diesel is a diesel engine system that includes active exhaust treatment for particulates and nitrogen oxides. Such a system is being pioneered by Mercedes-Benz.

◆ Fuel economy represents the Environmental Protection Agency (EPA) city and highway fuel economy ratings for the specified versions of each vehicle that has hybrid or alternative fuel capabilities.

◆ Price is a figure that is representative of what consumers are typically paying for each vehicle at retail dealerships. Depending on equipment and demand in your area, you may expect to pay somewhat more or less than that figure when you purchase such a vehicle. This is not an average of Manufacturer's Suggested Retail Price (MSRP), because such a price would not be helpful in the rather common instance in which hybrids sell for prices well in excess of MSRP.

◆ No electric vehicles, plug-in hybrids, diesel-electric hybrids, fuel cell vehicles, or hydrogen-powered internal combustion vehicles are covered in this chart for three reasons: they are not generally available to the public, they are not EPA-certified for fuel economy, and they are not being produced for the U.S. market by major auto manufacturers.

◆ Some vehicles in this chart, most notably a few of the Flex Fuel versions of vehicles from U.S. manufacturers, are available only to fleet customers. Because those policies can change, check with your local dealer to see if you can buy such a vehicle.

SEDANS

Brand	Model	Drive Type	Economy	Fuel Passengers	Price
Chevrolet	Impala	Flex Fuel	21/31	5	$22,000
Chevrolet	Monte Carlo	Flex Fuel	21/31	5	$23,000
Chrysler	300C	MDAF	17/25	5	$35,000
Chrysler	Sebring	Flex Fuel	24/32	5	$24,000
Dodge	Magnum	MDAF	17/25	5	$32,000
Dodge	Charger	MDAF	17/24	5	$33,000
Ford	Crown Victoria	Flex Fuel	17/25	6	$28,000
Honda	Civic Hybrid	Gas-elec hybrid	49/51	5	$25,000
Honda	Civic GX	Natural gas	28/39	5	$25,000
Honda	Accord	Gas-elec hybrid	25/34	5	$32,000
Lexus	GS 450h	Gas-elec hybrid	25/28	5	$56,000
Mercedes-Benz	E 320 Bluetec	Clean Diesel	26/37	5	$52,000
Mercury	Grand Marquis	Flex Fuel	17/25	5	$25,000
Nissan	Altima	Gas-elec hybrid	41/36	5	$27,000
Toyota	Camry	Gas-elec hybrid	40/38	5	$27,000
Toyota	Prius	Gas-elec hybrid	60/51	5	$23,000

continues

continued

Brand	Model	Drive Type	Economy	Fuel Passengers	Price
SUVs					
Chevrolet	Avalanche	Flex Fuel/MDAF	15/20	6	$35,000
Chevrolet	Suburban	Flex Fuel/MDAF	15/20	8	$40,000
Chevrolet	Tahoe	Flex Fuel/MDAF	15/21	8	$37,000
Chrysler	Aspen	Flex Fuel	14/19	7	$31,000
Dodge	Durango	Flex Fuel	14/19	7	$34,000
Ford	Escape	Gas-elec hybrid	36/31	5	$26,000
GMC	Yukon	Flex Fuel	15/21	8	$38,000
GMC	Yukon XL	Flex Fuel	15/20	8	$40,000
Jeep	Commander	Flex Fuel/MDAF	15/19	7	$35,000
Jeep	Grand Cherokee	Flex Fuel/MDAF	15/20	5	$36,000
Lexus	RX 400h	Gas-elec hybrid	32/27	5	$34,000
Mercury	Mariner	Gas-elec hybrid	32/29	5	$29,000
Nissan	Armada	Flex Fuel	13/19	7	$40,000
Saturn	Vue Green Line	Gas-elec hybrid	27/32	5	$23,000
Toyota	Highlander	Gas-elec hybrid	32/29	7	$29,000

Brand	Model	Drive Type	Economy	Fuel Passengers	Price
VANS					
Buick	Terraza	Flex Fuel	18/25	7	$28,000
Chevrolet	Express	Flex Fuel	14/18	8	$25,000
Chevrolet	Uplander	Flex Fuel	18/25	7	$23,000
Chrysler	Town & Country	Flex Fuel	18/25	7	$26,000
Dodge	Grand Caravan	Flex Fuel	19/26	7	$23,000
GMC	Savana	Flex Fuel	14/18	8	$26,000
Saturn	Relay	Flex Fuel	19/26	7	$24,000
PICKUPS					
Chevrolet	Silverado	Flex Fuel/MDAF	16/20	6	$27,000
Dodge	Dakota	Flex Fuel	16/22	5	$24,000
Dodge	Ram 1500	Flex Fuel/MDAF	14/19	6	$25,000
Ford	F-150	Flex Fuel	14/19	6	$28,000
GMC	Sierra	Flex Fuel/MDAF	16/20	6	$29,000
Nissan	Titan	Flex Fuel	14/18	6	$27,000

Index

G

W-X-Y-Z

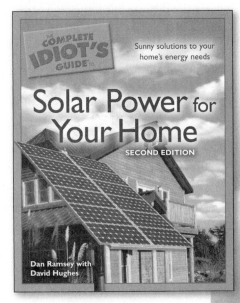